DREAMWALKER

Use Your Dreams to Make Confident Life Decisions

Patricia Rusch Duffey

© 2013 Patricia Rusch Duffey

ISBN: 150277108X
ISBN 13: 9781502771087

DEDICATION

This book is dedicated to all of you who appear in my dreams, whether you know you do or not. Especially you, George Clooney.

DISCLAIMER

For the most part, the dreams and descriptions included in this book use the real identity of the people involved. Occasionally I change a name to protect the privacy of those involved and avoid bringing up unpleasant discussions about incidents long forgotten by most.

TABLE OF CONTENTS

AUTHOR'S NOTES

For years I kept a dream journal strictly for my own use, not intending to ever share it with the public. After all, many of the images in one's dreams are quite personal. They might reveal things about yourself you wouldn't necessarily want all your friends and neighbors to know. I have had dreams about being naked in public places, having sex with celebrities, authority figures, and acquaintances, and committing crimes such as arson, theft, and even murder. Go ahead, admit it. You, too, have had dreams you'd rather not reveal to anyone. That doesn't mean you or I would ever actually perform the act described in the dream.

After noticing an intriguing trend within my dream journals, I shared a few of them with friends who I knew to be open minded or spiritual by nature. My dreams frequently "came true," or they had a sense of realism to them that couldn't be denied. One example: I would dream of a colleague inventing something grand, and a few days later he would bring up a startling new idea at work. It went well beyond coincidence, in my mind, so I started to pay closer attention.

At times I would have a hunch about something or some person. My internal radar registered uneasiness, and a few weeks later an unpleasant situation occurred.

These episodes were not always negative. On the pleasant side, I dreamed about a person coming to my rescue, and a day later she called me out of the blue.

My curiosity about these phenomena intensified when this would happen many months apart. There were instances in which I had a gut feel about a person the first time we met and dreamed about him occasionally. Two years later the person's true nature revealed itself, supporting my hunch. Sometimes it made me happy to see the real character of this person, and other times I would find myself saying, "I knew I couldn't trust him!"

Other times I dreamed about an idea and brought it up in a meeting or discussion, only to have colleagues dismiss the notion as unworkable. A year or two later someone else would bring up the same idea, and everyone applauded it as revolutionary. I remember a time before web sites became commonplace for companies to communicate with their customers. I dreamed about something that made me think we could create individual web portals for our customers to enter and see their names on the screen. *Hello, ARA Services: Please click here to see the products you have purchased from us.* One of the few web site developers at the time worked with me to create a comprehensive presentation of what needed to be done to bring it to fruition and presented it to my co-workers on the marketing team. The people in charge could not fathom how it would work, and it suffered a quick death. Eighteen months later we saw web sites appear with customized greetings, just as I envisioned.

It proved to me that gut feel, or intuition, is just as much a part of critical decision making as empirical evidence, facts, and figures. My dreams sent me messages to reinforce my feelings and in many cases alert me to things I hadn't even thought of yet.

Decades of watching this play out convinced me I stumbled upon a useful tool, not only at work, but in my personal life as well. In 2007 all the facts and figures we as Americans thought solid proved unreliable as hard working families lost their homes, jobs, and retirement programs. Government data depicted a rosy picture, while reality showed just the opposite in homes across the nation. I learned to rely on my instincts when the "facts" could not be trusted.

It is for this reason I wrote this book, hoping to encourage you, the reader, to use your own dreams to make confident decisions. I am convinced they hold the key to solutions for everyday problems as well as guidance for significant life strategies.

~ Patricia Rusch Duffey

INTRODUCTION

I am not a certified dream analyst. I hold no advanced degrees in psychology or metaphysics. If you are looking for basic information on what it means to dream of being caught naked in a crowded plaza with a tiger breathing down your neck, this is not your book. There are plenty of dream dictionaries and web sites, and most of them agree on the meanings of common images. They grace my bookshelf and are filled with green, pink and yellow highlights emphasizing the symbols most frequently appearing in my own dreams.

Perhaps I'm like you, if you became intrigued by dreams and nightmares at an early age and never lost interest. I keep a detailed journal of my dreams along with interpretive notes I feel are useful to me in life and decision making. These are my qualifications:

1. <u>Passion</u>. The stories emanating from dreams are magical. I find great pleasure in discussing them with others who believe in the wisdom inherent in dreams.
2. <u>Curiosity</u>. Psychology classes ranked high on my list of favorites in school. Studying Freud and Jung and their contemporaries stirred up in me an insatiable curiosity

about how the subconscious plays a role in daily living.

3. <u>Tenacity</u>. I do not forget dreams and the indelible impressions they leave. I rake through reference books and mull them over in my mind until the meaning becomes clear.

4. <u>Technical skills</u>. I write fast. In a later chapter I share my technique with you on how I am able to capture dream details before they leave my mind and glean the most from a dream before it becomes a distant memory.

I remember my first vivid dream waking me at around the age of six. Hearing my screams, my mother ran to my bedroom and discovered me sitting on the bed, knees to chest, hysterical about the snakes under my bed. For years the snake nightmare haunted me until I bought my first dream dictionary to learn the meaning behind the image. Snakes aren't always a bad thing in your dreams, and from a life-long herp-phobic, this is a significant admission.

The images revealed in one's dreams cannot be taken literally, according to dream analysis experts. The subconscious mind uses them to paint pictures that only have meaning once we apply our personal interpretation to the scene. A snake, for example, can represent a "snake in the grass," a person in your life who may not be what he or she seems. On the opposite end of the symbolism spectrum, the same serpent can represent healing. Look around the next time you are in a medical facility or reading health related publications. You may see the image of a snake wrapped around an upright rod. Its origin is in Greek mythology, and the figure is called the Rod of Asclepius. The god Asclepius is associated with healing and medicine.

There are a half dozen other interpretations of snakes in dreams, ranging from enhanced creativity to wisdom. The image is quite common. The purpose of this book is not to debate which metaphor is more widely accepted. The figurative meaning you personally place on something may differ radically from someone else's. It may take some time and practice to analyze the characters depicted in your own nighttime visions. Do the traits of the person that showed up in your dream represent something you admire or loathe in someone else? Or are they characteristic of you?

Commonly used idioms in our language also appear in dreams. Putting them in context will help you determine whether the expression should be taken literally. The snake is just one example.

Another example of a visual expression, a bit more abstract, is of a person wearing "an empty suit." The term is often used in the business world to deride someone deemed to be all talk, no action, without much substance. If this description fits someone in your dream, you are most likely making a judgment call on the individual rather than commenting on his attire.

An item that appears in my dreams is a suitcase. It would be tempting for me to look at it literally, as I traveled extensively during my corporate career. After seeing it appear in dream after dream, even when my travel slowed down, I realize it is emblematic of something else. Most of the time it represents some kind of "baggage" I am carrying around, figuratively speaking.

You may have dreamed of being naked or with your pants around your ankles. It could mean that you are afraid of being exposed, or you "got caught with your pants down." In my own dreams, one image can mean different things depending on my life's circumstances at that time.

Frequently my pastor will make an appearance. It does not necessarily mean that the pastor is literally involved in the situation described. I have learned after years of studying my journals that the pastor represents spirituality and provides me with a perspective rooted in my faith in God. Often I will analyze the pastor's role in the dream and realize the implied question is: "*What would Jesus do?*" in such circumstances.

In my dreams there is a definite spiritual aspect to deciphering their meaning. You may call it The

Universe, Supreme Being, The Holy One, Om, or The Divine. For me, it's God and the Holy Spirit. Whoever that is for you, I believe the deity sends messages through our dreams to help us determine right from wrong and provide a guiding light to choose the best path.

For nearly forty years I have kept a dream journal. It began unintentionally with simple notes in my pre-teen diaries. Having not yet been exposed to any dream dictionaries, my rudimentary "analysis" in my youth focused more on *how* I felt about the dream. Entries like "that was scary" or "what a cool dream" represented the extent of my dissection of dreams back then. As I read more books on the subject and shared my dreams with like-minded friends, it became clear to me that my subconscious was sending me messages on a regular basis. Just as friends and parents offer advice, dreams provide one more opinion to deepen our understanding of choices we make in life.

My parents, probably just like yours, had a favorite response whenever I wanted to discuss a particularly vexing teenage problem--"Do you think Connie or Carol should be my best friend? Will Kim be upset if I start riding home with Nancy and her brother? Does it seem like Cindy is out to get me? What do you think about my going to the dance with Scott?"   Mom and Dad would ask me a few clarification questions, relate a story from their own lives, and then hit me with the ultimate comeback: "Use your own good judgment."

No different than you, I tried to sharpen that skill to make proper life decisions. Many factors go into how well one does in that endeavor. Girlfriends, boyfriends, sisters and brothers, and well-meaning aunts, uncles, and grandparents weigh in on issues of the day. As I grew up, guidance counselors, pastors, and teachers played meaningful roles in helping me choose the right course of action. There seemed to be another force at play, too, letting me know when a decision I made felt right. It centered in my gut. I could physically tell when I made a bad judgment call.

Decisions became more consequential as I finished school and entered the work force. The challenge of working as a female in male-dominated industries presented daily decision-making opportunities capable of making or breaking a career. The stakes were higher. My circle of personal advisors expanded to meet the call for sound counsel.

I read every self-help and leadership book by renowned gurus I could get my hands on. I formed allegiances with "the right people." I took personality tests and met with psychologists who explained my strengths and suggested areas for improvement. I developed relationships with other women who experienced the same workplace challenges as I, and they became my personal board of directors.

Yet, even with legions of support, I kept going back to my intuition when faced with a big decision. When all the experts and friends counseled one way or the other, my gut cast the final vote. I share in the following chapters how I developed my sixth sense through the use of dreams and believe you can learn to do the same.

With perhaps the exception of your Higher Power, there is nobody who knows more about you than yourself. Dreams speak to your subconscious. For centuries experts have postulated that they are a way to tap into your psyche to uncover your deepest thoughts. After studying over a thousand of my own dreams spanning more than thirty years, I have come to trust them as my most accurate internal barometers.

An exciting aspect of dreaming is making a thought your reality. You can do anything in dreams. An average business executive turns into Superman. Tone deaf hummers see themselves on stage as operatic singers. Human beings fly without airplanes. You can guide your own destiny by utilizing thoughts and ideas surfacing through dreams.

According to WebMD, in a study of *Personality and Individual Differences,* people who are imaginative or creative tend to remember their dreams more than others. We draw on our inner resources for inspiration in problem solving, and our dreams play a key role. Whether or not you categorize yourself this way, you can sharpen your skill in using dreams in a practical way. Start by turning up the dial on your attention meter. To help you, I will provide excerpts of dreams from my journal, originally dismissed as silly until I took a deeper look.

Making a conscious effort to understand the messages in your dreams will pay off by helping you solve problems that challenge you in waking hours. I lay my head on the pillow and ask for answers to come to me. Piecing together the images the morning after a vivid dream is gratifying when I realize the answer to my question is right there.

This book is intended to give you practical examples of how I use scenarios from my dreams to help me feel more comfortable about decisions I make with regard to problems and opportunities facing me each day. My journal will always hold a special spot in the night stand, ready to capture messages missed during waking hours. I share personal victories and struggles, all influenced in some way by a dream.

As you move through the chapters, you will note some paragraphs are in italics. These entries are taken directly from my dream journals over the past three decades. I chose to include them exactly as scribbled in my mind's morning fog so as not to lose the nuances which contributed to my interpretation.

The intimations of the night are divine, me thinks.

~ Henry David Thoreau

GUT CHECK

Above all else, trust your gut. It is advice I have repeated over the years to employees, protégés, friends and colleagues as they waffled over significant decisions about work or relationships. *It* never fails *me*, but sometimes I fail myself. I have a lifetime of stories about times I did not follow my own advice, rationalized away a gut feeling, and regretted it. I occasionally tossed aside my parents' advice to "use my best judgment," opting instead to second guess myself or fall prey to someone else's influence, even when my instincts told me I was making a mistake.

What is a gut feeling? It is a knot in your stomach that feels as though you swallowed a baseball. It sits there in foul territory waiting for an outfielder to pick it up and throw it back to the pitcher. It won't roll back by itself. Your rational mind—the outfielder—can make a play or wait for someone else to make a move.

According to *Psychology Today* gut feel is a "mental matching game" where the brain rifles through its files of past activities, recollections, knowledge and emotion to come up with a way to process whatever is going on. The most reliable gut feelings, then, should be those that are based on years of experience, keen insight and vivid memories. How could anyone capture all that information and put it into a useable form? Would it not be useful to have a computer to collect all that data, put it through a cleansing process, and produce a gut-check rating before you act on something? Score a ten on the gut-check meter? Good score, go for it; but if you score two on the gut gauge, you better do some more homework.

The good news is this supercomputer exists. I call it my "gutometer." It is a dream journal, and it performs the role of data processor very nicely.

My experience leads me to believe "gut feel" is simply a physical manifestation of intuition, the awareness or knowledge of something without hard substantiation to support it. My intuition is usually trustworthy by itself, but my analytical left brain constantly wants to test it for reliability. Oftentimes, there is no direct information to support or refute a feeling, but my gut will express loud support or physically exert caution. Rather than suppress it or rationalize it away, I have learned to let my dreams offer a second opinion.

Case in point: Barry, a good friend and colleague, had an important decision to make about a career move within our company. During his decision-making process he shared his desires with another co-worker, Chaz, and mentioned it to me. I immediately sensed this might not be a wise move for his career. It ranked about an eight on the gutometer.

"Are you sure you can trust him?" I asked Barry. He and Chaz had been friends for several years. He dismissed my apprehension and continued bringing Chaz into his deliberations. My intuitive red flag shot up when I had a dramatic dream:

> *We were at a group function. There was a cage and Barry was inside of it. He was holding onto a poisonous snake—a black water moccasin. Suddenly the snake recoiled and snapped. It bit his hand and people started screaming. We all started discussing written rules about*

*how we were going to prevent that
from happening the next time.*

I did not share this dream with Barry, but I had a distinct feeling the snake in the dream represented Chaz. I did not act on my gut feel that Barry made a crucial mistake by confiding in Chaz. This dream scored a ten on my gutometer.

A few weeks later office chatter revealed Chaz went to see the boss and laid out his argument for why he should be considered for the job Barry wanted. Barry already discussed his desire for the position with decision makers in the company. Chaz, to assist his own negotiations with the powers-that-be, betrayed Barry, and used the information and private background Barry shared with him in his own job pursuit. I felt sick for Barry and did not rub salt into his wounds. The experience confirmed my gut—backed up by the water moccasin dream—had not failed me. I failed to use it to help a friend.

A second dream about the same characters six weeks later raised the red flag of intuition once again, convincing me this time to reinforce my cautionary advice to Barry.

My dream: *Barry, another friend, Pat, and I were walking on a beach. We saw a guy hang gliding, dangling from a balloon, and I told Barry and Pat to look up, that it was probably Chaz because he had told everyone if he received a promotion he would make speeches and address the group from a balloon. Barry ignored him, focusing instead on some luggage he had left in the hotel. We went in to get it and passed a TV with a beautiful woman on the screen, and they were showing a close-up of her breasts. I was appalled they would do that and called it to Barry and Pat's attention. They had not even noticed it because they were grousing about the luggage.*

My interpretation of this dream is that Barry and his friend, Pat, were so busy paying attention to other things they did not see the glaringly obvious. They never noticed the buxom woman on TV or the man hang gliding. This metaphorically told me Barry missed what happened right in front of his face. Chaz was after his job.

Furthermore, the metaphor of the luggage told me Barry carried some baggage of his own preventing him from clearly seeing Chaz's true motive.

All along I felt Barry made a mistake about sharing so much personal information with "the water moccasin." Chaz, "flying high," celebrated his triumph.

You cannot always convince your friends to follow a path based on your own dreams, a lesson learned whenever I share a dream with a non-believer, and they dismiss it as silly or coincidental. Do not let that stop you. Messages from your subconscious hold great importance. For me, the two dreams served as a warning not to share too much of my own confidential career plans with Chaz. I tucked a note in my cerebral file cabinet. It served me well months later when I found myself in a similar decision-making situation. I did not bring Chaz into my circle of trust. Those two vivid dreams assured me of the soundness of my advice to Barry. Gut check and checkmate.

Intuition has been studied since the 1400s. Science is full of examples in which intuition played a key role in an important discovery. In Chapter 2, I share stories about well known historical figures whose Eureka! moments originated with ideas gleaned from dreams.

Jonas Salk, the developer of the polio vaccine, is an outstanding example of a scientist who combined the art of intuition with his analytical side to reveal patterns that led to important discoveries. In a 1991 interview he talked about his book, *The Anatomy of Reality: Merging of Intuition and Reason*. "Reason alone will not serve. Intuition alone can be improved by reason, but reason alone without intuition can easily lead the wrong way. They both are necessary. The way I like to put it is while I might have an intuition about something, I send it over to the reason department. Then after I've checked it out in the reason department, I send it back to the intuition department to make sure that it's still all right."

His analogy of sending a hypothesis back and forth between "departments" reminds me of my own need to test my gut feelings by sleeping on them.

Since dreams harbor the deepest subconscious thoughts, it stands to reason this is where unspoken ruminations and observations made during the course of our day manifest themselves. All the experience, memories and insight captured in the minds of dreamers tend to bubble up and present themselves as an idea, a hunch, or intuition. John Maynard Keynes, the famous economist, said, referring to the discoverer of gravity, "(Isaac) Newton owed his success to his muscles of intuition. Newton's powers of intuition were the strongest and most enduring with which a man has ever been gifted."

I would like to believe my intuition is one-hundred percent correct one-hundred percent of the time. Yet, I have an analytical streak that makes me demand extra assurance. Scientists and researchers verify their hunches using an orderly process to test a hypothesis. I utilize my dream journal.

Messages appear in my dreams to confirm my gut feel about a person or a situation. Have you ever felt uneasy about someone and later discovered out he had a criminal background? Maybe you dreamed about a catastrophic event you providentially could have avoided.

I experienced something similar with someone who invited me to his wedding in Hawaii. Dick's fiancé, Anny, seemed to be a nice woman, but I observed a few interactions between them which raised my antennae just a bit. He seemed a little preoccupied the day before the wedding. Nothing significant happened, and the wedding went off as planned. The night of the wedding, however, I dreamed Dick had been in an accident, ending up in "ICU." At the time I did not give it a second thought, but recorded it on the hotel stationary to add to my collection of dreams. It turned out to be prophetic.

Unfortunately the marriage did not last, and later I learned Dick went through a difficult time as he harbored doubts about the marriage even on his wedding day. Had I paid close enough attention to it right away, the dream may have alerted me to Dick's need for "intensive care." Fast forward a decade or so, and all of this came to light as I read through my journals one day.

Journaling is a tool recommended by life coaches and counselors to help you gain insight into your life by recording your thoughts and insights. Life coach Joy Huntsman (Joy and Associates) teaches The 45-Day Journaling Challenge that encourages people to realize their goals by discovering who they are inside.

Online web sites such as MyTherapyJournal.com have introduced ways to get started journaling and organize yourself to stay with it long enough to see benefits. I decided years ago to journal with a focus on dreams because some of my best thinking is done in the middle of the night.

If you choose to follow my path, I highly recommend reviewing your dream journal from time to time. Patterns emerge, and, if you connect the dots correctly, warnings and "ahas" leap off the page when you look at it in the light of a new day. When rediscovering the intensive-care-unit dream I looked further back to see if I missed other clues about Dick's situation. There were, indeed. This next journal entry, dated two weeks prior to the wedding, essentially predicted a rough ride for the couple. I wish I took the time to piece things together.

Tom (my husband) and I were on vacation in a place similar to Disneyworld. The hotel was under construction. Each time I went in the elevator I stopped on two top floors where there were indoor pools and groups of ethnic dancers practicing poolside. One of the elevators was on the outside of the building. It was a wobbly scaffold with ropes. I yelled for Dick and Anny to stop and get off. Tom and I went across the street to go on a roller coaster. We were deciding which car to get in and it was one by itself, not hooked up to the others. The guy told us it was waiting for the rest of them. Tom started to get in but I said no, that it did not look safe. We all went to the next line of cars and they were all floating in water. We sat in the car and the water came up to our faces.

Benefiting from hindsight and the ICU dream, I realized The Universe (God) tried to send up a flare once before. The description fit Hawaii—a place similar to Disneyworld with ethnic dancers (hula?) poolside. A wobbly elevator, unsafe roller coaster and water up to our necks combined to paint the canvas ultimately revealed when Dick and Anny split up. I started to realize how instrumental dreams could be for practical purposes. Unsure whether I could have prevented Dick's pain, at least I would have been there as moral support.

My gut feel manifested itself similarly several years ago when another friend, Diedre, announced her engagement to a man I knew from professional circles, albeit not well. My gut reaction surprised me. Dread is how I would characterize my initial response when she told me of their upcoming nuptials. I suppressed it but was not the least bit surprised when I dreamed about their impending marriage.

I was walking the streets of Chicago and decided to go into a bridal shop. In came my friend Diedre, and she started talking about getting married. I started to look for a dress to wear to her wedding, when a thought popped into my head that she might not invite me to the wedding. The entire dream had a dark, dreary look to it, like a heavy industrial city. Many people from a women's club came in and out of the shop.

I kept my thoughts to myself and did not attend Diedre's wedding. I sent a gift and supported her outwardly. It came as no surprise, however, when several months later she shared with a small group of friends who belonged to the same women's organization the unimaginable nightmare she lived with her new husband. She endured a long, painful divorce. At times like these I wish my gut feel and supporting dreams were not so in sync. It left me with a feeling of helplessness mixed with regret that I didn't tell her about the dream.

My intuition just prior to my niece's birth told me my sister might have some issues with her pregnancy. A little older than most new mothers, she told me about the precautions her doctor suggested. Her due date was originally December 7. On October 24 I had this dream:

Dreamed that Sandy (my sister) had her arms full and I offered to hold the baby. It was in a little dustpan, so I carried it around. I picked it up by hand and accidentally dropped it in a narrow container of hot water. Dad was there and yelled at me to get it out. I dunked my hand in, but it was so hot. I finally got her out, but there were little tiny doll clothes and one shoe floating in there. I looked at the baby, and it turned into a bottle of thick shampoo or lotion. It wouldn't pour out. I shook the bottle several times and tried to cool it down. Finally it turned back into a baby again. I was pretty upset about it.

I felt sick thinking something might be wrong with the baby once she arrived. My niece came earlier than expected, on November 11. As many "premies" do, Kinsey stayed in the hospital several days. Her bilirubin count soared, blood sugar dropped, and she slept in the intensive care unit where I peaked at her through the window. After five long agonizing days, my niece "turned into a baby again." My dream painted images of difficulties Kinsey would endure during her first few days on earth.

Gratefully, no frightening dreams preceded the birth of my four nephews over the next decade.

Everyone has intuitive abilities. I have consulted with intuitive counselors on occasion, and it is clear to me these skills are like muscles. You develop them the more you use them and get better with years of practice.

It is the same with dream interpretation. You can pick up a dream dictionary and use it to analyze the symbols that appear in your nightly visions. The real benefit comes when you figure out what those symbols mean to you, as they will differ by individual. It takes discipline and diligence to keep a detailed journal along with your analyses and do it consistently enough to create a useful tool.

The power of intuition supported by dream messaging can offer you reliable guidance for making importance decisions for your life. I have a gut feel about that.

2

THE DREAM BOX

The chronicles of my dream life reside in a tomato-red, wooden box, eight by fourteen, six inches deep. When I started recording my dreams decades ago, I did not intend to organize them for any purpose other than my own amusement. If I knew their eventual purpose, I would have written them all in bound journals, numbered them consecutively, and placed them on the same shelf to be pulled out whenever I needed guidance. That's how I normally do things, in an organized fashion. Instead, I tossed them here and there.

Somewhat out of character for me, I did not prepare for journalizing dreams on a regular basis. My job kept me traveling extensively, so packing light formed my routine. The roller bag had no room for a bound journal. Hotel notepads became my platform for recording thoughts arriving in the middle of the night. Housekeepers probably wondered how I could go through so many of them in a two-night stay.

At first some of the little notes ended up in my nightstand drawer upon my return home, as it seemed to be an appropriate place. The drawers on bedside stands, as a rule, are narrow and shallow, so soon mine overflowed with Marriott, Hilton and Sheraton pads. I needed to find a better solution. Browsing through a vintage shop one day, the charming red box called out to me, and so it became home for the thousands of scraps of paper making up the lion's share of my journals.

When I decided to write this book, I took one look at the wooden box and wondered where to begin. The task seemed enormous. Every note needed to be transcribed, as they were written in shorthand. (More about that in Chapter 5.) One page of shorthand notes could sometimes morph into three pages, typed.

You could liken the process of transcribing the dream journal to a six-month reunion at which people pour over scrapbooks, photo albums, and home movies, reliving the times recorded for posterity. As I typed, I remembered nearly all of them and could recall the images vividly. It brought back memories of career phases, personal trials and tribulations, and friends and family who since passed. It turned out to be a project worth doing, whether or not I chose to write the book.

During the years when I traveled less extensively and took the time to be more disciplined, I wrote in traditional bound journals, recording my dreams in chronological order of their appearance. However, the red box will keep its status as *the* dream vault for the foreseeable future, or until I can no longer squeeze in another Marriott pad under the lid.

3

HISTORICAL DREAMERS

Whether you think there's a supernatural aspect to dream analysis or agree dreams have a practical use, those of us who practice it are in good company. There are countless precedents of famous dreamers who used their nocturnal subconscious to create works of art, solve perplexing problems of the time, or avert death and disaster.

From Charles Dickens and Salvador Dali to Rene Descartes to Olympic hurdler Edwin Moses, reports of dreams contributing to practical problem solving have been recorded in history. Mathematical equations, the Periodic Table of Elements, and masterpieces in art and music claim their origins in dreams.

Here are the stories of some favorites of mine, including Biblical figures, one of the "Fab Four," a United States president, and a certified genius.

Daniel

One of my favorite books in the Bible tells the story of Daniel who lived in ancient Babylon. King Nebuchadnezzar, the second and arguably most important king of Babylon, asked for his soldiers to bring him some of the best looking, strongest, and smartest men available to serve in his kingdom. Daniel and his friends, Shadrach, Meshach, and Abednego were brought to the king. He wanted to show them favor, so he offered them the finest food, meat and wine he served to his own people.

Daniel and his buddies followed God's direction and turned it down, saying, "No, thank you, King, we will have vegetables and water instead and see how we fare." They did well; God showed them favor, and they were given special skills. (Now that's a powerful testament for eating your veggies, but I'll leave that for another book.)

God gave Daniel the ability to interpret dreams.

The king started to have some strange dreams. He asked for all the astrologers, magicians, and psychics in the kingdom to guess the dream itself and then tell him what it meant, or he would cut them up and destroy their homes. If they could guess the dream and its meaning, the king promised he would bestow upon them gifts. The astrologers and wise men protested, telling the king nobody could guess his dream.

So the king sent his soldiers out to kill every one of them. Daniel prayed about it, and God provided the answer he needed. Daniel went to the king and revealed his dream, an image of a statue made from precious metals, iron, and clay, summarily destroyed by a large rock. He explained to Nebuchadnezzar the dream's prediction of kingdoms to come, with The Kingdom of God prevailing. Daniel's interpretation satisfied the king, and he became a favored servant. His buddies were also spared. Dream analysis skills paid off for Daniel and his friends.

Later Daniel shifted from interpreting others' dreams to analyzing his own. Numerous visions outlined in the Bible predict the future for kingdoms and countries. The most revealing of Daniel's dreams, according to Biblical experts, foretells the end of times.

I do believe a Higher Power utilizes dreams to send messages to its believers. If wise men from thousands of years ago utilized their analytical talent to save lives, I think it is a skill worth honing in today's world.

Pontius Pilates' wife

For ages people believed God sent messages in dreams. Pontius Pilate, leader of Judea during ancient Roman rule, is best known as the man officially responsible for crucifying Jesus of Nazareth. His wife warned him to leave Jesus alone. According to the Bible in Matthew 27:19, the unnamed woman sent her husband a message as he deliberated Jesus' fate: "Do not have anything to do with that innocent man, for I have suffered a great deal today in a dream because of him." Pilate dismissed her advice, and the rest, as they say, is history.

When my better half tells me about his dreams, I pay attention. It might be filled with valuable insight into what is going on in his mind.

Albert Einstein

The Theory of Relativity—which details how speed and time are related—is a complex principle of physics. It certainly changed the world for physicists, engineers, and scientists, and it came to Einstein in a dream. Einstein dreamed he tumbled down a mountain, faster and faster, and as he looked to the sky, what he saw in the stars gave him the idea for the theory, $E=MC^2$.

In later chapters I share a few examples of ideas that came to me in the middle of night. Genius? I would not go that far, but practical for my job at the time, definitely.

Elias Howe

The key to the modern sewing machine eluded Elias Howe in the mid 1800s until he had a horrific dream leading to his "aha" moment. He dreamed of being captured by savages, placed into a big pot of boiling water, and poked with spears. Each spear had a hole in the tip. As he analyzed his dream the next morning he thought about needles poking into garments just as the spears jabbed at him in the nightmare. He altered his design, and voila!

An image so vivid is something I would not dismiss lightly. I dreamed one time about a giant bird landing on my hand and looking me in the eye. A bird in the hand....

Paul McCartney

Sir Paul was quoted regarding one of his most famous compositions, *Yesterday*. "I woke up with a lovely tune in my head. I thought, 'That's great, I wonder what that is?' There was an upright piano next to me, to the right of the bed by the window. I got out of bed, sat at the piano, found G, found F sharp minor 7th — and that leads you through then to B to E minor, and finally back to E. It all leads forward logically. I liked the melody a lot, but because I had dreamed it, I couldn't believe I had written it. I thought, 'No, I have never written anything like this before.' But I had the tune, which was the most magic thing!"

Can you imagine dreaming a masterpiece such as this beautiful song?

I am no McCartney or Einstein but have dreamed in a similar way many times, coming up with ideas for work or home projects. Many times I will wake up and draw a picture of the idea along with a description of it.

During a time when I worked in the bakery industry, I dreamed about buying jumbo muffins in a food court. In the fuzzy moments of awakening, I drew a picture of the muffins piled high on a cart. My artwork was abominable (I have never professed to be an artist), but the idea seemed solid.

Two years later, while working in another company, the idea came to fruition when we started marketing a muffin cart to supermarket bakeries. The stores did an outstanding job selling muffins to consumers with this display method. The seed had been planted long ago in my subconscious and sprouted at just the right time.

Another time I dreamed about two chefs with whom I worked, creating bite-size goodies to serve before meals. The tasty treats were chocolate and vanilla. I came up with a list of names for them including Twin Bites, Twin Kisses, Sensory Twins, Nuggets, Twin Nuggets, and Chocolate Nuggets.

I never did anything with it, as my job responsibilities veered off in another direction. In some ways I wish I still worked in the bakery business, because the names sound clever to me even now and might be a tremendous marketing opportunity. To protect my intellectual property, I hereby declare this dream occurred on June 8, 2003. Perhaps the idea will show up in a future consulting proposal.

Abraham Lincoln

The 2012 film *Lincoln* reminds us President Abraham Lincoln may have actually dreamed about his own death just days before the assassination. There is some debate about the assertion, but it is documented that Lincoln shared his dreams with cabinet members and his wife, Mary. One account claims the president told his cabinet he dreamed of sailing across an unknown body of water at great speed. He also apparently revealed he had the same dream repeatedly on previous occasions, before "nearly every great and important event of the War."

Two weeks before his death he dreamed he heard someone crying, went to investigate and saw a man lying in a coffin. When he asked guards about the identity of the deceased man, they told him it was the president.

Like Lincoln, there have been numerous providential dreams recorded in my journal. I share some examples with you in Chapter 8 Premonitions.

Joseph

Joseph, another man from the Bible, is the lead character in an intriguing story of sibling rivalry. He is also the title character in the Broadway play *Joseph and The Amazing Technicolor Dreamcoat*. I hope his story does not prevent you from sharing your dreams with your own brothers and sisters. Joseph's brothers bullied and abused him because their father treated Joseph as his favorite. One day Joseph told his brothers he dreamed he ruled over them and they bowed down to him.

The dream did not endear him to his covetous siblings. The brothers sold Joseph, a Jew, as a slave to Potiphar, a high ranking Egyptian palace official. Potiphar's wife took a liking to the good looking Joseph and tried to seduce him. He spurned her advances, and as a result was thrown into prison where, ironically enough, he spent time interpreting more dreams.

The Pharaoh heard about his abilities and asked Joseph to interpret one of his strange dreams. Pharaoh already consulted Egypt's resident astrologers, who came up empty when asked to explain the meaning behind his unusual vision. He complimented Joseph on his skill. Joseph responded, "It is not me. God will give Pharaoh a favorable response."

Pharaoh shared his dream image with Joseph: Pharaoh stood at the bank of a river and saw seven fat, well fed cows emerge from the water. Right after them came seven other cows, lean and not doing so well. The seven ill cows ate up the well fed cows, but they did not fare any better.

Days later his dream continued. He saw seven ears of prime corn come up in one stalk. Right after them came seven withered and thin ears of corn. The thin ears devoured the seven good ears.

Joseph prophetically predicted this meant there would be seven years of good crops followed by seven years of famine. He advised Pharaoh to stock up and get ready for the seven lean years. Pharaoh did so and put Joseph in charge of the food pantry so he could use his knowledge in managing the crisis. It is a classic example of utilizing dreams for everyday problem solving.

You see, Pharaoh's dream had two different metaphors--cows and corn--both with the same divine message. Get ready for seven long and depressing years, Joseph told him. God gave him fair warning by way of his dreams.

Joseph did such a good job interpreting dreams, Pharaoh put him in charge of the entire kingdom. If you remember the story or the Broadway play, Joseph eventually used his power to help his family during the famine. His skill in interpreting dreams brought him personal prosperity when Pharaoh appointed him to lead the kingdom, and he saved his family and community as well.

Each of these famous characters used their dream analysis skills for practical purposes. Saving lives, protecting wealth, and developing new products and processes are useful applications of messages conveyed in a dream. Whether or not your dreams become part of literature or folklore matters not. What does count is whether you pay close enough attention to the ideas, thoughts, and potential strategies revealing themselves to you in the middle of the night to turn them into practical and productive action plans.

4

DREAMING IN COLOR

The basics of dream symbolism are widely accepted by those in the business of interpretation. The images displayed in dreams are not to be taken literally. They speak metaphorically about emotions and thoughts that lie deep in the subconscious. Thousands of years of analysis have established certain images to be quite common among dreamers.

You, too, have probably had your share of being chased or falling in a dream. Flying without an airplane or missing a flight are common themes I have discussed with friends who share my analytical interests. I established in the Introduction my tendency to dream about snakes, another familiar symbol. Others dream frequently of animals, perhaps reflecting their own character traits mirroring those of the animal depicted. I discuss themes in more detail in Chapter 6 Dream Themes.

It surprised me as I reviewed more than a thousand dreams to find a number of recurring images and patterns, unapparent until I looked at the collection in its entirety. One thing missed earlier jumped off the pages--my use of brilliant colors.

My journaling tendency is to include enough detail in my descriptions of people, places and things to produce a clear picture when reading it back later. Some excerpts read like this:

> *They invited me over for meat that tasted like wine and it was purple in color.*

> *He had a butch haircut and wore yellow glasses that looked like Elton John's.*

> *Inside the house was a black grand piano on one end, and on the other end were five white rocking chairs arranged in a circle.*

> *I opened the closet door and in it were dozens of tiny black binoculars and odd little opera glasses.*

I completely glossed over my inclusion of colors. In the examples above, purple, yellow, black and white emerged. Looking at my dreams in the aggregate, I found patterns. Three colors appear most often. Just as interesting as the colors that do appear, are the ones I would expect to dream about, but rarely do.

The most frequently appearing hue in my dreams is without a doubt blue-green or teal. A truly beautiful color, in my opinion, some experts say teal signifies desirable traits such as trustworthiness and loyalty. Where these traits exist in people within my subconscious, I paint them in dreamy teal.

According to Sleep Culture, "Teal can signify you have a journey ahead. These dreams could also indicate thrift and 'fine harvest' which can be interpreted as positive for any undertaking."

As is common in searching for meaning in dreams, opposing points of view on what teal represents exists. According to Dream Bible, teal represents "fear, jealousy, greed, guilt or an insensitive attitude towards a positive change." That is a whole different story than a fine harvest. So what is a person to glean from two widely differing opinions?

To extract the most usable meaning, one must put everything into context within its own set of circumstances. This is why it is helpful to view an image with a similar description in more than one dream, or you may be led in a direction opposite of what was intended.

Take, for example, a dream about two co-workers who accompanied me to an event. At the end of the evening when they left the building, each entered her respective limo. Jane got into a black limo and Linda, a teal limo. The dream continued as I stood there deciding which vehicle to choose, and a gangster emerged from the black limo. I, of course, chose the teal limo. Looking at this dream individually, I would deem Linda to be a trustworthy associate, designated by the color of her teal limo. However, is one dream enough to make a judgment?

When placing the teal-limo dream next to other dreams about Linda, more favorable images emerge, and together they tell me she is someone to be trusted.

I dreamed of a friend's wedding, and in the receiving line everyone wore a teal dress.

Unlike some of my prophetic dreams about impending doom for some marriages, this one looked to be a winner, bathed in the color of trustworthiness. The couple is still happily married.

Improving on the validity of my analysis, I find many references to teal in dreams, enough to make a solid determination of what the color signifies in my world. Here is another entry from my journal:

> *I bought some shoes in the color teal for everybody. I did not get any for mom though. When I gave the shoes out to everyone, they tried them on and liked them. Then I was embarrassed and ran to the store next door. I bought a size 7 teal tennis shoe for mom and ran back and told her I had forgotten to give them to her. She tried them on and they were way too small. I tried them on and they fit me. I said maybe I should just keep them, but then I changed my mind because they were a cheap version. I picked up the shoes and ran to the store to exchange them.*

It was when I ran out that I saw Candace in her shoes, and we started to fly.

In waking life, Candace and I bonded as the only women in a sea of managerial testosterone at our company. She is also a dream believer. We enjoyed sharing our dreams with one another and analyzing the messages within them. It did not surprise me that she became the recipient of the beautiful blue-green shoes.

The teal in this dream painted an uplifting picture of us finding our freedom in the professional world, something not readily accessible to women of my mother's age. As the old saying goes, "if the shoe fits...." The freedom inherent in the teal shoe image did not fit my mother.

Yellow is another color capable of displaying radically different meanings. It showed up often enough in my dreams to warrant further study to determine its meaning.

Some colors take on the meaning common in our culture. Yellow is universally recognized as a caution sign, such as a yellow traffic light or the yellow flag in a NASCAR race. It is also a slang term some use for one who is cowardly. Dream Moods offers this explanation of yellow, "If the dream is an unpleasant one, then the color represents deceit, disgrace, betrayal, cowardice and sickness."

On a more positive note, yellow is bright like the sun and could represent an ability to shine in a dream setting. It is the second most common color appearing in my dream world.

A professional acquaintance, Paul, is a successful businessman and a risk taker. This colorful dream featuring yellow sent me a direct message during a time I felt stagnated in achieving sales goals I set for myself.

> *Paul was driving an SUV and I was sitting in the back. He was driving on a yellow boardwalk. He would go a short distance and then the yellow boardwalk would drop and he would stop. If he went a foot more he would fall off the end. Then another piece of the boardwalk would come up and he would drive a little farther. He*

kept doing that. We were in the air over water headed for a beach. It was nerve wracking. We eventually made it to the beach but it was a scary ride along the way.

The boardwalk, painted in yellow, represented my own trepidation, not Paul's. He is fearless. True to his risk-taking nature, he pushed a little at a time until he reached the beach. I needed to let go of my fear and learn a lesson from Paul. The practical application of a dream like this for me would be to make a list of more aggressive goals and go for it.

Yellow takes on a cautionary tone in a dream about my father with a bittersweet ending. We discussed investment strategies during my weekly calls to him halfway across the country. During one Sunday call, he told me he decided to put some of his money into a new fund, something a little out of the ordinary for the average investor. He studied it for some time and read newsletters about the plan which he sent to me. I reviewed them to learn about the opportunity and its potential downside. A dream recorded around this time may seem a bit graphic in its description, but notice the rich metaphors and the placement of the color yellow in this journal entry.

> *Dad was doing surgery on some small pigs. He sliced them open and put his hand in behind a bunch of stuff looking for something that he was calling bacon – it was like a slab of ribs. If he found it, the pig was sewn back up. If it was not there it was no good and the piglet was put in a pile to be destroyed. He checked some pigs, and then he turned them all over to me. I cringed when I put my hand inside the piglet, and then I ran over and laid the bacon on my bed. It had a bright yellow bedspread and there was blood all over the place.*

Bringing home the bacon—an idiom commonly used to refer to earning money—seemed to be the headline in this excerpt. The yellow bedspread illustrated my own cautionary demeanor, and the bloody scene appeared to be a potential "blood bath" from the financial risk.

The dream image came into focus. The investment strategy paid off for my dad, but I wondered whether I should take the risk. If I did, it might be "a bloodbath."

I had a conversation with my father's investment advisor after Dad passed away. He characterized Dad as a shrewd investor and complimented his approach to balancing risk and reward. I recalled this dream and retrieved it from my journal as a reminder of the mysterious guidance sometimes dispatched to me in the middle of the night. The message received from it told me I might reap financial gains from doing what my father did, and I took the step with the same financial advisor and did not regret it.

Pink is the other color gracing my journal on frequent occasions. As with teal and yellow, it can run the spectrum from negative to positive in interpretation. Affection, love, and kindness are represented by pink surroundings, but so are immaturity and weakness. Culturally, to receive a pink slip means you have been terminated from a position, so it could signify the end to something in the metaphorical images of a dream. I once dreamed about a colleague,

Steve, wearing a pink shirt shortly before he announced his retirement.

Shades of pink throughout my dreams indicated significance for me, as it is not a particular favorite of mine. Pink could play a compelling role in communicating, if you think about the pink phone slips used for years in office settings. They were all about giving someone a message.

I recorded a dream shortly after taking a position at a new company. I knew my fellow employees for many years, but not as co-workers. The imagery of this dream, and in particular the color pink, highlighted a concern about my new boss and the culture he established at the company. As it turned out, this dream foreshadowed an eye-opening experience for me while employed there.

Dreamed I was being tested by a psychologist or psychiatrist for my job. They were hooking me up to wires and called this "in session." I was there more than a couple of times. I was with a bunch of people who were mixed up. They were just friends that suddenly took a turn and started doing weird things. A guy that looked like Robert (my boss) nudged me and said "this is how they get when they start having a spell." Then that person would be hauled off for a session. In one scene I was in a pool and we quickly got out because it was time to go to the doctor's office. Robert asked a couple of us if we had gotten anything done. I answered no, that we were all in session. He rolled his eyes like it was taking too long for us to dry off. I saw some friends on a balcony at the hotel and waved to them. When they saw me I pointed to my sweater and shouted that it was pink and that was supposed to be the way they would find me. I told them that people I thought were normal were all getting treated for some kind of mental thing.

For a visual person like me, a dream like this one etches itself in my memory because of the addition of a color. The weaker side of pink—immaturity and instability—seemed to take center stage. It painted a picture of a dysfunctional office in which people acted strangely and "needed therapy" to deal with the despotic leader. In real life, it did not take long to find out how close the dream came to describing the actual culture of the company I joined. Practically speaking, I learned how to live with it, as my job was fairly autonomous and I knew I wouldn't stay there very long. Having the truth revealed to me in a dream gave me an odd sense of comfort, perhaps because the devil you know is preferable to one who behaves unpredictably.

Green is my favorite color. It, too, can have both positive and negative implications and cultural connotations such as things related to the environment. Green with envy comes to mind as an image that might appear in people's dreams. On the negative side, green can indicate materialism (love of money), selfishness and deception. The color rarely shows up in my dreams.

In over a thousand dreams in my journal, there were only a few references to green, and those literally had to do with golf courses or landscaping.

I have learned in the thirty-year review of my journals that dream analysis must be a perpetual practice if you want to be able to incorporate it into daily decision making and problem solving. Today I am content with "all things green," even though the hue is conspicuously absent from my dreams. Tomorrow I may light up the night in emeralds. The mystery of nightly meditations intrigues me, and even after so many years of analysis, I continue to discover things about myself.

5

PRACTICAL PROBLEM SOLVING

My thirty-plus years of dream journaling solidified my theory that dreams can be a useful tool for everyday decision making and problem solving. The key is to find a way to keep track of your dreams which allows for analysis with the benefit of hindsight. After a while, confidence builds and so does clarity in making decisions based on the information revealed.

Putting a little discipline in place helped me analyze my thousands of dreams as a practical tool for everything from relationship building to career counseling. Here are some of the habits I've established to capture the messages being sent to me on a regular basis:

1. Diligently journal your dreams as soon as you wake up before anything has the ability to impact your memory. Completely dark rooms are great for sleeping, but once you turn the light on, your dreams tend to scurry away. Just like that, they are gone. I keep a book

light in the night stand to illuminate the journal ever so slightly—just enough to see the page and make sure the ink in the pen is flowing.

I have a secret weapon that has served me well, helping me write quickly before the memory fades. It is called Gregg Shorthand. For over forty years I have used it to record everything from shopping lists to meeting minutes to diaries. There are other options available today to help you get the information down quickly such as voice recorders and smart phones. My shorthand is such a well perfected skill for me that I do not want to mess up a good thing, so I stick with it. The other action I recommend to capture the dream in its entirety is to tell somebody as soon as you wake up, but do not let telling about it substitute for writing it down, as nobody cares about the details of your dreams as much as you will.

Another tip: Do not carry on a conversation with anyone about another topic until you have finished your journal entry. Train your sleep partner to leave you alone until your pen stops moving. Interruptions will abruptly erase your memory, which can be especially frustrating when you have had a real doozy.

2. Be specific with vivid details. Note the colors of things and describe clearly how a person's face looked or what she wore. If you can think of a comparison, for example, "Elton John glasses," write it down. These clues are invaluable later when you are trying to determine the emotion being revealed.

   I dream specific names—Joe Canneloni, for example. Whether or not I know a Joe Canneloni is irrelevant at the time of the dream, but it is important to record it, nonetheless. Years later a very similar name or connection may come up in real life. Having dreamed about it in the past proves interesting, if not prophetic. I once dreamed about someone named David Zastrow. I never knew anyone by this name. Here's the dream and what happened later:

Dreamed that I was going home from a meeting. We were expected to be in Washington DC and we were going to be late. We ended up getting a ride on a truck that was full of military and government stuff. A guy named David Zastrow invited us to ride with him in this truck. It was going to Washington DC as well. There were guns in there and lots of communications equipment. I kept thinking they probably like to have civilians in these trucks so they do not get attacked. There was a counter and people were doing their emails. I was on my blackberry and I kept thinking that this would be a good time for me to lay out all my plans for a website. I called somebody; I think it was Juliet [sister in law], to tell her that we weren't going to be there as early as we thought, but that we were getting a free ride and it would be good for expenses. David Zastrow was watching people in the truck and somebody was messing with the blinds to keep the sun out. I realized that he was watching to see that nobody messed with a little microphone that was tucked inside the blinds.

An eerie feeling crept over me while searching social media sites to see whether David Zastrow connected to a previous chapter in my life. He did not, from what I could determine. However, his name did show up on a list of employees for Northrup Grumman, a well known military defense contractor. Cue the spooky music.

3. After recording the dream itself, write down what you *think* it means. In my review of over a thousand journal

entries, the vast majority of what I wrote at the time was on target, given the benefit of hindsight. Equally revealing were the dreams I interpreted incorrectly at the time. In most of these situations, I simply dismissed them as not having much meaning. Twenty years of retrospective convinced me that in reality they were telling me something to which I should have paid much more attention.

4. Find a trusted friend with whom you can talk about your dreams. My co-worker and friend, Candace, and I would greet each other at the office first thing each morning and share the dreams we had the night before, offering opinions on how to interpret them. It may have seemed like so much water-cooler talk to those who overheard us, but they were practical and productive sessions in helping me determine what my nightly thoughts were trying to tell me.

Your buddy may not be your sleep partner or spouse. In years of sharing my dream passion with friends of the same mindset, we all lamented the fact that our significant others were less than interested in what we dreamed. In fact, most of them dismissed us as silly or our dreams as bizarre rather than useful. Ignore the naysayers and dream on.

Not every dream points to monumental life-changing decisions. Some simply provide practical and useful guidance for simple or mundane problem solving. At times my dreams centered around chaotic events or depicted me in a disorganized state. I knew from recognizing the symbolism that they referred to something going on in my life or job that needed work before it would be ready to unveil. A simple but telling example:

Dreamed that I needed to go and see a foodservice distribution company, so I drove there to look for a couple people in their healthcare department. I couldn't remember their names. A woman came out and started tearing my car apart. They brought out fabric, and it looked like they were going to recover it inside. I watched for a while and then got nervous because my meeting was to start in a minute. I got in the car and drove it while it was all torn up. Somebody told me I needed to see the president named Nick. I drove right inside the building and was parking in the hallway when I thought better of it and tried to move the vehicle outside.

From a practical standpoint, this dream helped immensely. My job at the time focused on putting together distribution programs, and I was working on a healthcare project mentioned in the dream. The woman tearing my car apart represented this distributor "tearing my program apart."

For me to not remember a name is highly unusual, because it is a skill I have honed ever since my years as a high school teacher. After giving it some thought, I realized the forgotten names belonged to people I should have included in my correspondence, but had not.

Driving the car into the building, as if delivering the program, and waiting to see Nick were both big red flags for me. Nick was actually the name of one of my own employees. His appearance reminded me it would be a good idea to consult "my Nick" or his department to complete the program. Offering practical advice, this dream provided my final checklist before "driving the program through" to the customer.

One more example of problem solving through a dream occurred right around the time I considered making personnel changes in my organization. The following nighttime vision clearly told me there were people who were preventing our team from soaring to new heights. Here is how it went:

> *Dreamed I could fly a corporate jet. I took it out for one ride, and it was pretty smooth. I had a couple people in the plane with me. The plane lifted off quickly and was very easy to handle. The second time, though, I gathered a bunch of people who wanted to go for a ride. They got in. I started to take off, but the plane was too low. All of a sudden tall downtown buildings were in front of me, and I had to abruptly bring it up to a*

nearly vertical position to get over the buildings. (A woman) riding with me said she was going to throw up and screamed for me to stop. I finally got over the buildings and flew around for a while. When I came back and landed it seemed like the airport was small, and the plane was tough to land.

My gut had been warning me about one individual in my organization who did not "have the stomach" for the changes we made to our marketing and sales plan. I felt she may be weighing us down, as she put up roadblocks each time I asked her to alter her plans to align them with the new strategy. The dream provided another valuable gut check in my thought process about the organization. It signaled for me the need to have a conversation with her.

I happen to be one who does not believe a coincidence is strictly a chance event, a fluke, good or bad luck. My friend, Margaret, and I discussed a 1998 dream that acted as a personnel reference of sorts. When I first had the dream, I did not think much of it until I shared it with her, and she revealed something that knocked my socks off.

My dream centered around a business trip Margaret, a sales rep named Sherry, and I took to San Francisco. Sherry stayed in the Allerton Hotel in my dream, and Margaret registered at the Alvin Hotel. It's not unusual for me to dream specific names of places whether I know them or not. In fact, it is rarer for me to not dream names and places, whether they are real or made-up.

In the dream, the Allerton turned out to be a rough hotel, with no phones and a baggage carousel that went around and around without letting anyone grab their bags. The Alvin, on the other hand, gleamed as a fine hotel with exemplary service. When I shared the dream with Margaret, she laughed at the coincidence. She told me that a few days before she talked with someone in the company's operations department who provided great service assisting her with an issue. She sang his praises and said if I ever needed assistance from Operations, to call this gentleman. His name? Rich Alvin. He earned a top spot on my phone list, because my dream told me Alvin offered *first class service*.

Some examples I share about how I have utilized dreams to make decisions may seem trivial. When you make hundreds of decisions a day at your job, it helps to have a little voice pointing you in the right direction, rendering a gut check, so I'll take all the help I can get. One of the key tasks assigned to my department might fall into the mundane category—choosing sites for meetings and events. If you make the "wrong" choice, however, it will quickly show up as one of the top ten most important decisions made for that event.

If you have ever been involved in the planning of a conference or large scale gathering in your business, you know it can be a thankless task. Someone will always be unhappy because of the bad hotel beds, terrible food, or distance from the airport. Forget one little detail such as picking up the president at the airport, and you can be on his black list for a year or until one more meeting goes by without a hiccup. Your entire reputation as a meeting coordinator can hinge on whether you choose the right location for one meeting.

I enjoyed plowing through details with my two sidekicks—Mary, event coordinator, and Susan, travel agent. A dream I shared with them at a planning meeting had all three of us rolling on the floor laughing our....well, you get the idea. The dream went like this:

> *My nephew ran home to get me and said the neighbors were fighting because of some trees on their property. A big fight broke out, and I decided to intervene. We went inside the neighbor's house. She had a cat. It looked like a Halloween cat with an arched back, really scruffy looking and big. It was almost like a wildcat. He jumped at me, and I tried to hit it so it wouldn't hurt me. The house was on Schuylkill Road.*

Before any mention of the dream, Susan spread out several brochures from properties we were going to consider for our road show. I opened up the first brochure and shrieked. Susan and Mary almost fell off their chairs as I explained my concern about choosing that particular hotel. Its location—Schuykill Road! What we didn't need was a fight breaking out or the bad luck of a Halloween cat overshadowing our meeting plans. We chose another property.

Months later Mary and I stood knee deep in plans for a meeting to be held in Reno. I lent my support, going over checklists two or three times to be sure we nailed down every detail. We tried to anticipate every possible glitch and put preventive plans in place. Yet, one region manager, Steve, always seemed to encounter problems with his flights. I nearly forgot his history when I had this dream:

> *We were on a small plane and it kept getting stuck in the water off the runway near a clump of trees. We kept saying if we could just get it to go over the trees we could get to Reno. Finally the plane got high enough to get over the trees, and then Mary jumped out of the plane and ran into a janitor's closet to start mopping up the mess it had left. Meanwhile, I was on the phone with Steve [the region manager] and he told me he had a problem with his flights. I was angry that it was him again. I was pleasant to Steve and told him we would take care of it. Then I hung up and ran after Mary saying I*

couldn't believe we screwed up Steve's trip again. Of all people, we do that to him each time! I couldn't find Mary because apparently she was hiding, but finally I found her in the janitor's closet.

Sound silly? Perhaps, but looking at the practical side of dream analysis, it saved Mary and me time, trouble, and aggravation by reminding us to double check Steve's flights to Reno. We needed to avoid Mary having to *mop up a mess*. We did just that, and fortunately, he attended the meeting without a hitch.

Have you ever taken on a task and spent so much time trying to achieve excellence it teetered towards disaster? I admit to being a perfectionist, especially when the project may be high profile. I strive to turn out the best product possible. In a well functioning committee or work group, someone will eventually suggest "it is good enough." My tendency is to ask the members of the group to step back and try to see the project through the eyes of the customer or user. Try to capture their thoughts and add them to yours to create the perfect end result.

I recall the example of a training course I created as the manager of a new department established to support sales people. It is based on the concept of consulting with customers versus convincing them to buy a product. One of the people on my development team continued to say she could not grasp the consultative selling concept. We wrestled with the curriculum, trying to find a way to explain it that would make sense. This dream provided helpful direction.

> *Dreamed that Susan and I conducted a seminar. We invited people to a 4-hour session that had all of our products as well as those that weren't ours. The products included Crayolas, paper, scissors, and knives. We invited a customer to speak at the first session. Seven or eight people showed up, and we charged them to be there. We made $21. The second seminar, on another day, had 22 people show up. We were excited, but when we took our first break, we lost some people. The second break we lost more. Susan got up to speak. The*

audience started talking amongst themselves and getting up for food. I told her to move on so we wouldn't lose anyone else. When I walked around I saw the book we had put together, and it had pictures of how to cut up vegetables and fruit. It was simple stuff like cutting up lemon wedges. Just then my boss came by, and I was excited to tell him we had 22 people there, but I critiqued it and said we did way too much talking. I overheard a couple people who escaped say they did not want to listen to us talk all day. We need to shut up and let the people do the work.

The direction I gleaned from this dream seemed to be just what we needed to break through our creative block. I set two objectives, both of which seemed obvious to me after the dream appeared.

First, we needed to put more participant interaction into the plan. Working with the training company experts, we came up with role-play scenarios mirroring real sales calls for our company. Conclusion: cut the lectures and involve the sales people.

Secondly, the materials must fit the real world. The dream pointed out a workbook full of lemon wedges, not the products being sold—Crayolas and supplies. In real life, the workbooks supplied by the training company contained generic examples of consultative selling. They did the job for the most part, but the curriculum came alive when we decided to customize it using real life examples from our industry. If we were to sell Crayolas, the dream guides said, use them in the workbook exercises.

It took a few more weeks than we planned to complete the project, but the final outcome reinforced the right decision to customize the program. The salespeople learned new concepts and enjoyed going through the course.

Utilizing dreams for a "gut-ometer" works for practical problem solving whether it has to do with work, personal, or civic responsibilities. One of my most rewarding professional experiences resulted from joining the Women's Foodservice Forum in its early stages of formation. The association, established in the late eighties to advance women's careers in the industry, departed from the typical trade group. Fresh thinking, collaboration, and devotion to a common cause bonded board members to each other as we poured time and effort into building the organization.

Like many institutions, the WFF encountered bumps in the road, but our shared passion for the mission enabled us to weather many storms. Shortly after celebrating our ten-year anniversary the group prepared to elect a new chair. At our board meeting one woman, Stella, spoke out about nearly every issue. She monopolized the conversation, clearly looking like a campaigner for the seat. I caught the sideways glance of my good friend, Caroline, a fellow board member. She and I did not speak out loud, but privately after the meeting we shared our concerns about this person.

Our instincts kicked in when Stella gave a speech, talking about taking the organization in a new direction. She framed it around management principles and long-term strategic planning, so it sounded good to the general audience. Caroline and I were not so sure. We felt it veered from the original mission of WFF.

Fortuitously, during the trip to attend the board meeting, I had this dream:

The board members were in downtown Chicago at a hotel and needed to go to another building. Thinking I knew my directions, I got on my bike and headed out. Got to the building and Lena and Derek [fellow board members] were there. Another strange woman was there, but I didn't know who she was. We were at a garage that works on cars and Derek said he could really use some pieces that were lying in a box. I said I could carry them in a bag and strap it on my back, still riding my bike. He put a filter and two or three other greasy things into a thermal bag with cross straps on it. I put it on my back and got on the bike. The stuff was so heavy the bike started to lose its shape. The handle bars came close together, more like a rowing machine. The pedals did not work well. I was all crunched up. I started riding thinking I would see downtown and the hotel. We rode for a while and suddenly we were in the outskirts of the city. I could see downtown, but it was far away. Derek asked if we should get a cab, and I said it isn't that far. The strange woman said she knew a poem that would help us figure out where we were. She started reciting it.

At first glance this dream does not seem to have one ounce of connection to the board meeting. It is superb justification for journalizing in detail while your mind is fresh. The dream featured unusual images, so I read it repeatedly in an attempt to figure out the message it tried to tell me. The "aha" moment came when I broke down the symbols one by one.

A key sentence in the description: *The stuff was so heavy the bike started to lose its shape.* I went through it step by step.

1. What does a bike represent? A means to get to where you are going.
2. What happens when something loses its shape? You do not recognize the original.
3. What caused the breakdown? Stuff (baggage, greasy dirty stuff)

My next step is to figure out who or what the bike represented. Breaking it down one image at a time, revealing symbolism pointed to the board meeting and the organization, starting with the location. At the time, Chicago served as headquarters for the WFF. Downtown represents the heart of the organization. Another clue is the presence of Lena and Derek, veteran board members who shared the original mission we established ten years before. It made sense that this dream centered on the Women's Foodservice Forum.

The dirty items being loaded into the bag characterized an undesirable load to carry. Thinking back to Stella's diatribe, I remembered that she listed everything she believed needed to be fixed within the organization. Most of the other board members had been there since the group began, and we were proud of all our accomplishments. We didn't see the "dirty, greasy" load. Sure, we   issues, but they were all a natural part of building an organization.

The finger pointed directly at Stella as the problem, not the association. The bike losing its shape told me we stood to lose our core, the original values we espoused to bring the group successfully to its ten-year anniversary.

Continuing to piece the images together, the strange woman in the dream portrayed Stella, I believe. In the dream, she recited a poem, indicating she could speak eloquently, as she did the previous day in front of the board. She captured everyone's attention.

One clue in the dream, a bit more abstract, clarified the message for me even further. *I could see downtown, but it was far away.* Her approach skirted the organization's mission, but missed the vision; it would not further the interests of the group.

Apparently my fellow board members came to a similar conclusion. In the coming months alternative candidates emerged for the chair position, and the board elected someone other than Stella. I felt confident about the decision.

6

DREAM THEMES

Dream dictionaries provide valuable and interesting interpretations of the symbols showing up in our nightly narratives. Snakes, for example, may reveal fear of commitment, sexuality issues, or alert you to a "snake in the grass" with whom you are dealing. Showing up naked in inappropriate places might mean you are afraid of being exposed or see yourself as vulnerable in some way. Several of my dream buddies share with me their recurring dreams about trying to fly without the use of an airplane. Flying dreams are very common, especially among people who consider themselves to be imaginative.

I, too, have my share of repeats. Some scenarios stop appearing after a while. The benefit of journalizing dreams for an extended period of time gives me twenty-twenty hindsight, helping me understand why certain subjects repeat themselves and what causes others to cease. It took several years for me to realize that when an issue resolved itself, the repeating theme having to do with that issue stopped appearing in my dreams.

Since my teens I have dreamed about running along, flapping my arms, and lifting off the ground to enjoy a birdseye view of the world around me. My flight path tended to be just above the buildings.

Disturbing to me, though, is my feet drooped down, bumping into things on the rooftops. A host of experts might interpret this as a joyous experience of soaring free. My own assessment, however, zeroes in on my feet. Bumping into things clearly represents the obstacles I have faced in different phases of my career. Notably, my feet bump into buildings which to me signify corporations. Managing through the "good old boys" network at a time when few women were advancing in my industry is probably the biggest hindrance in my recollection. Politics, bosses and lack of financial power could have been posted on top of the buildings in my dreams, and as I flew over them I "stubbed my toe" along the way.

According to Dream Moods, "Having difficulties staying in flight indicates a lack of power in controlling your own circumstances.

You may be struggling to stay aloft or stay on set course. Things like power lines, trees, or mountains may be obstacles you encounter in flight. These obstacles symbolize something or someone who is standing in your way in your waking life. You need to identify what or who is trying to prevent you from moving forward. Difficulty flying may also be an indication of a lack of confidence or some hesitation on your part. You need to believe in yourself and not be afraid."

Who does not encounter obstacles at some point in his career or personal life? I do not necessarily see this as a negative. In fact, I am delighted the issue is exposed in a dream because it focuses my attention on it. Now I know what to watch for in order to determine ways to overcome the issue.

A combination of self reflection and other dreams of mine offer clues to what may be standing in my way. I share several of the dreams in other chapters. In reviewing my journal, I realize this theme stopped somewhere in the five years following my decision to go into business for myself. The timing is not a mystery. It coincides with my feeling of gaining control over my own destiny.

I traveled extensively at times for business purposes, suitcases and briefcases in hand. It does not surprise me when the image of baggage reappears in dreams over the years, but not necessarily referring to my real-world activities. The allegory, "carrying a lot of baggage," provides a striking illustration of issues and people weighing me down. Whenever my dreams dredge up this image, I know I need to think about the subject to move forward unencumbered. An example is this dream in which I had too many bags to deal with, leaving things in a mess:

> I was in an airport and had my large brown suitcase and golf clubs. I checked the clubs and went back to find my bag where I left it, and it was gone. I ran all over the airport trying to find the bag. It was hidden upstairs, and the guy at the counter told me it was in the area but he wouldn't tell me more. Later in the dream I had a purse that I left on a counter at a stadium. I kept a small purse with me. I decided I had better not leave the large purse, so I turned around

to get it and noticed that a security person or housekeeper had it. She wanted my ID. Luckily in my small purse I had a business card with my name on it, and I found a car rental document that had my address on it. She went through the large purse and finally matched things and gave me the purse. I had to walk through a large parking lot to find Sandy [sister] and Nancy [close friend.] I dropped some things in the parking lot and tried to move ID into two purses. I was juggling a lot of things and kept thinking to myself that I had to tell Sandy never to leave her things unattended. I kept misplacing bags and leaving them alone when I should have been watching them.

As I analyzed it, my first thought went to the ID, and I wondered whether I might be having some sort of identity crisis. Yet I dismissed that thought since my job seemed to be going well at the time. I established myself in the foodservice industry with credibility and felt as if I knew my purpose at the time. So why would I have been juggling so many bags?

Taking a step back to look at the bigger picture, I realized it may have nothing to do with work. The day before this dream took place the Iraqi war, President George W. Bush announced the commencement of Desert Storm. Sleep escaped me, as my head bobbed in front of the television screen, watching scud missiles destroy their targets.

War is unsettling on its own, but add to it the hassle factor of traveling with new airport restrictions taking the fun out of it, and it increases the stress factor. Practically speaking, there is not much one individual can do about the war in Iraq from a sofa in Minnesota. Or maybe there is. I could turn off the television and tune in Mozart, take up yoga or meditation, or find another way to manage the stress.

One other clue is the color of the suitcase—brown. Tony Crisp's *Dream Dictionary* says brown can depict gloominess.

I firmly believe dreams provide a valuable tool alerting one to personal overload. They provide clues to help manage life and make decisions, but it is important to put them into context by stepping back and looking at the bigger picture.

This is not the only time I've dreamed about bags. Looking back over my journals revealed a pattern of similar visions. A few weeks earlier I dreamed about a co-worker helping me carry my bags. Another one a few days before portrayed me opening a suitcase and discovering a pile of jewelry inside. Jewelry usually depicts spirituality or wisdom in dreams. Taken together, this series of dreams with a common theme told me something brewed beneath the surface. What else in my life contributed to a feeling of lugging around too much weight?

I reread the large brown suitcase journal entry, looking for a clue. My sister, Sandy, and good friend, Nancy, appeared in the episode. Could it have something to do with family issues? Then it hit me. Two months before the dream doctors diagnosed our father with lung cancer. He underwent surgery to remove part of his lung, and my mother, a retired nurse, had her work cut out for her caring for him.

Mom endured her own health issues, having endured two heart bypass surgeries eighteen years apart. This would be as difficult on her as on Dad, dealing with the newest crisis. I looked at the dream journal again. *I had to tell Sandy never to leave her things unattended.* My subconscious mind, through dreams, alerted me we needed to step up and attend to Mom and Dad. Sandy, with a busy job and a four-year old at home, could only do so much. My brother also had young children pulling him in every direction. I admonished myself for not calling home more often and made a renewed effort to check in at least weekly.

Baggage shows up at times when I feel as though I am carrying a huge load at work or at home, such as it did in this dream:

> *Ken [a co-worker] and I were on the road and much of the dream found me trying to stuff things back into my briefcase and it wouldn't fit. He and I were meeting at the airport and he picked up his baggage, but not mine, so I had loads to carry.*

I know when I see more than one dream like this in a short period of time it is time to rebalance my priorities or stop taking on so much responsibility. My personal self-development objective is to learn not to overcommit my time and resources. This type of dream is a gentle reminder of my goal.

Gentle is good if I'm listening carefully, but sometimes my dream gods feel the need to use graphic images to get my attention. Here is a good example of that.

Dreamed I was in Chicago doing presentations with work people and we were due to check out. Had tons of luggage and nothing was packed very well. I had to get about 10 different things together, and there were little bags that did not fit inside the big ones. Jim was there and he was supposed to get our luggage from the bell captain and call a cab, but they lost it. I was working on a presentation and writing things on a pillow case because I did not want to take out anything else. I knew we had to get to the airport so I started gathering my things. I ran for the elevator with all this stuff and even a bunch of flowers. I got inside the elevator, and Jim called out that I forgot one small bag, a toiletry case. He threw it to me in the elevator. When I unzipped it there was underwear all balled up inside, and it was Jim's.

Once again, the luggage theme appears to tell me I am trying to do too much. The image repeats itself so often during a particular three-month period, I instinctively knew the message being sent.

The image of little bags not fitting into the big ones represents details I may be forgetting. The story used a marketing technique to make things look good even if the details were missing in the presentation. The flowers represented my attempt to make it pretty, if not substantial. Writing my presentation on a pillow case makes sense because it's one way to process something I am working on—I sleep on it.

In addition to the overstuffed suitcase alert, the dream revealed another tidbit of information regarding my feelings about Jim. As a colleague in the real world, he had not earned my trust or respect for various reasons. Usually dreaming about underwear depicts a person revealing something of himself. In this dream he simply threw another bag at me, full of his dirty laundry. Unfortunately, this image did nothing to elevate him in my mind. I saw him as part of the problem.

There may be a temptation to interpret dream themes literally because it comes quickly to mind, but I urge you to pay attention to the potential hidden meanings. Dreaming you are conducting a symphony does not necessarily mean it is in your future, even if you do fancy yourself as Leonard Bernstein's heir apparent. It might mean you need to *orchestrate* an event or paradigm shift.

Golf is a good example. It could be tempting to believe a golfing dream is literally about my skill on the links, especially when I am playing frequently. However, at certain times in my career, the golf theme took on a completely different meaning.

During the early years of climbing the corporate ladder, I repeatedly dreamed about being at or around golf courses; in fact, often I would be running through them trying to find my way out. Ever since my first marketing job working for a golf car company, the game presented challenges. For women in business, golf renders an internal struggle. It is the quintessential good-old-boys' club. Business is conducted on the golf course, and if a woman does not play, she is left out of meaningful relationship-building opportunities with customers. I have talked about this with dozens of non-golfer friends who feel they are deliberately being left out when a male colleague schedules a golf game with a customer. It gives you a competitive advantage if you play.

As you read the following dream pay close attention to the words I chose for this journal entry. In hindsight they revealed a thought pattern prevalent in my world of work.

> *I was attending a conference at a resort, and we were playing in a golf outing after the last session. I had to go back to my room to get my golf things and got lost. I cut through the golf course and ended up in a sand trap. Two teenagers*

came up to me and said I couldn't cut through, but I kept running. I knew I still had a long way to go, but a guy called out my name and said to come with him. I asked him to run my way because I was late. Another guy came up and was going to arrest me. They kept paging my name. I finally got to the clubhouse and a woman helped me when I told her I needed clubs. I was worried because I had not been back to my room and did not have any of the things I needed like a hat, sunscreen, socks, and shoes. They were going to help me catch up to my group which was four holes into the round. While I was waiting, the woman had sympathy for me and said if I was a man they wouldn't have treated me like that. She said they were ticked off because last year I won the longest drive contest, and they couldn't believe a woman did that.

Were you able to pick up the symbolism? The dream is rich with metaphors, beginning with the sand trap, a common hazard on a golf course. In my dream it stands for the inherent traps women fall into when working in a male dominated environment. Lacking political savvy, taking things too personally, or forgetting to leave disagreements in the boardroom are just a few examples. The image stored itself in my subconscious because I could relate. It painted a vivid illustration of the message I needed to receive at that point in life.

Losing your way is a frequent concern when navigating the course of business whether you are male or female. Fortunate are those who find a trusted mentor to provide guidance. Coaches who offered help to me in waking life are represented by the teenagers (someone younger than I) I met on the dream course.

Another guy came up and was going to arrest me. Arrest me—or is he trying to arrest my progress? It raised my red intuition flag.

On the encouraging side, another man "runs my way," possibly exemplifying a colleague with mutual goals.

Did you notice I did not have all the tools to be successful? It was a woman who helped me out with clubs and expressed her empathy. I thought about women colleagues who might be sources of support.

In the dream I tried to catch up with the group, suggesting the need to run much faster to stay up with everyone else in the game.

Why would my golfing buddies leave me behind? Because it is their way of competing. They did not expect me to be any good at what I did, but "I won the longest drive contest."

Are you getting the picture? By breaking down the dream one image at a time it becomes easier to relate it to a possible message hidden behind the painting. If you do it often enough, you will improve your skill at finding the meaning for your own life. The bottom line is the dream used golf clichés to give me a heads-up on potential issues in the workplace and hint at possible solutions. It's an extremely useful theme for me.

My advice to you is to pay careful attention to the double meanings and metaphors creeping into your dreams. Avoid dismissing something as simply a venue for your dream to take place. By journalizing your dream immediately after waking up, you will be able to capture details helpful in your analysis.

In another dream well over a year later, I dreamed of receiving a memo written to "The Men of 55". The memo contained straight forward information, with a separate page listing my name. It required me to answer twenty questions before revealing the content of the memo. My journal read:

> *When I went to the guy who had written it, I pretended I liked the idea of these guys getting together and asking me questions. It was clear the group was set up to counter everything that women were trying to do within the company.*

Once again the concept of being treated differently than the men cropped up. The timing of the dream provides a clue as to why this image appeared when it did. At this point in my career, I had successfully negotiated my way into the male dominated workplace and proven myself. For several months an intensely competitive environment existed as the company worked its way through integration of a newly acquired business. Jobs were being doled out and people were jockeying for position in the new structure. I did not feel I received fair treatment. My subconscious thoughts of being held back because of my gender surfaced in the middle of the night.

The name of the group—The Men of 55—referred to my co-workers. Our offices were located on Highway 55.

One recurring and vexing theme centers around being unprepared, and there are two ways it manifests itself in the middle of the night. One portrays me as an ill-equipped teacher in front of her class, making things up because I do not have the correct information available. As a former high school and college instructor, it feels all too familiar.

I remember, nearly forty years ago, my first day of teaching a two-hour high school consumer education class. It took weeks of preparation, because there were no textbooks to follow, so I created my own curriculum. The students arrived for class, eager to learn. I launched into my lesson plan feeling the exuberance of becoming a business education teacher.

Thirty minutes into the class I completed my lesson plan and looked up at the clock. There were still ninety minutes to go, and I ran out of information. It went down in history as my first experience in thinking on my feet. I came up with a game to play illustrating the talking points from the lesson and breathed a sigh of relief when the bell rang eons later. What could have been debilitating circumstances turned out fine, but the idea of being unprepared haunts me to this day. It is no surprise it thrusts itself into my dreams occasionally, just like it did this night, twenty-four years after the unnerving consumer education class episode.

Dreamed that I became a teacher again and I was totally unprepared for class. The class was full. I had to stand on top of a riser to be seen, and then it got higher as if I was standing on top of a desk. I had little pieces of paper, and I was looking at them to help me. I told the class we would start with me telling them something about myself. I said I had been a teacher years ago and thought it would be fulfilling to do it again. I kept dropping the notes. I came up with a good idea to kill some time. I went around the room and asked each student to say something about himself and how much experience he had in typing. I did that and people started talking, but I was not listening because I was trying to figure out what I was going to do for the rest of the time in class.

Even today, while writing this, I feel the dread crawling up my spine at the recollection. The timing of this dream is paramount. Office matters were normal, and nothing particularly stressful dominated my personal life. I happened to be attending a meeting which included many people from out of town. My management teammates and I were well prepared to lead the meeting. The date I dreamed it: September 12, 2001.

Do you remember what you did the first few days following that horrific day in the history of the United States? We were thrust into a new normal. People walked around in a catatonic state for days. As a country we needed every ounce of strength and calm we could muster.

I thought this dream reached back twenty-five years for a reason. It urged me to organize in some way to contribute to our collective sanity. The memory of being exposed and unprepared flooded back. My instincts kicked in, and I, along with my colleagues encouraged our group to try and do something ordinary. Think on our feet. Kill time until the bell rings. Inch forward.

We robotically moved ahead with our agenda items, knowing full well nothing would be accomplished, yet craving a return to the mundane world we used to know. We golfed an eerily quiet round without the white noise of airplanes flying overhead. Fiercely scribbling in my dream journal, it helped me process the paranoid thoughts boiling up from beneath my forced composure.

Not only did I need to think on my feet and prepare for the work day, but I joined the rest of the country in thinking about readying ourselves in basic security.

The notion of vulnerability is my personal fear to conquer. Journalizing dreams comforts me by acting as a tool to process anxiety and fear into action, allowing me to feel in control.

The idea of being unprepared manifests itself in a second common dream theme. For as long as I can remember, and verified in my journals, the metaphorical theme of a band or orchestra plays a recurring role in my subconscious. If I am dealing with a work project or a personal decision, and I am feeling ill prepared, it may appear in my dreams in a musical group setting.

I play the French horn, not professionally, but I have for more than forty-five years, so the routine of what to do in a performance is second nature to me. When I dream about a botched performance or chaotic orchestra set-up, I know instinctively to pay attention.

The theme manifests itself in several creative ways. At times I am seated with the rest of the band, looking up at the conductor as he raises his arms to begin, and then I realize I have no instrument. Other times the horn may be there, but I will look at the music stand and find there is nothing there. Since these dreams occur more than occasionally, they are as revealing to me as the classroom dream.

An absent horn conveys to me that I do not have the proper tools in place for whatever project—work or otherwise—I'm involved in. Missing the sheet music connotes a lack of instructions or a plan. Perhaps more information is needed to make a looming personal or professional decision. The image of a conductor flapping his arms wildly or not keeping a steady tempo tells me I am in dire need of direction from some authority (maybe even me.)

One of the most distressing, yet insightful, band dreams came to me at a time when I carried the weight of the world on my shoulders. A business deal hung on by threads and my financial wellbeing might be sorely tested. This dream, unfortunately, did not immediately bolster my spirits. However, it did make me sit back and take a deeper look at what I could do to remedy the situation.

Our band was playing to a full stadium. I had two sets of music, one with normal notes on it, and the other had strange symbols and circles all over it. I was switching back and forth between the two, and it was very confusing. When it came time for the Stars and Stripes, we played up to the climax and suddenly everyone quit playing. Tony [the director] looked at us, nobody was playing, and so I timidly played about six notes of the line and then realized it did not sound very good alone. People started piling out of the stadium. Some of the musicians got up and left. I picked up a blanket and started hugging it. On the other side of the stage I saw Morgan [a long time co-worker and friend] and I ran up to him to give him a hug. I said I missed him, and he said everything would be ok.

I awoke admonishing myself, wondering how in the world we could forget how to play Stars and Stripes. Most of us have played it since we were kids. At first glance a scene like this signals a red alert, but look closer at the symbolism in the last half of the dream, and a rosier picture emerges.

I picked up a blanket and started hugging it. Metaphorically speaking, this one is fairly obvious—I clutched a security blanket. (Picture Linus of the Peanuts comic strip.) All I had to do is figure out where in real life it existed or who it might be.

Secondly, one of my "advisors" came by in the dream to reassure me. (More about these characters in Chapter 13 Advisory Board.) The person appearing on stage, Morgan, is a friend and former colleague who experienced some of the same ups and downs I did in corporate settings.

I viewed Morgan as an extremely positive person. He shared with me over the years some of his difficulties early in life, but he turned things around when he turned his life to Christ. Whenever I needed a boost, I would call Morgan to hear his cheery voice. I recognized his appearance in the dream as reassurance and a blessing.

The dream scene in which I started to play by myself and did not sound very good signaled my need for support. If I could surround myself with the right people, my burden would be lifted. I put my conclusions into action by reaching out for assistance from friends and family. My financial turmoil did not turn around overnight, but I found comfort in the support extended to me by good and compassionate people. Without a nudge from my dream, I may have delayed asking for help, adding to my stress.

The process I use for studying dreams like this may be useful for anyone's personal analysis. Take your time. Do not be too quick to jump on the most obvious meaning and make it your truth. I nearly interpreted the dream to mean all is lost. Instead, it pointed me to a solution as I read it several more times and unearthed its positive perspective. Patience and deliberate examination of all your dream-like images will result in an emerging picture full of meaning and direction.

Not every dream requires several readings to ascertain the message. Sometimes an orchestra dream hits me right in the face with its message. An employer of mine had been taken over by an investment group, and we were in the early stages of learning whether this would be business as usual (as new owners always purport in the beginning) or whether we should start dusting off our resumes.

I dreamed of being invited to dinner by some people and several odd things happened, one of which was pizza being served in cups rather than plates. Another unusual element— the background music emanating from the speakers in the restaurant. French horns were playing a raucous piece, and I noted in the journal I did not recognize the song.

As the real-life company drama played itself out, this dream made sense. The new owners were taking us in a direction few of us supported. *We did not recognize the song they were playing.* In fact, we did not see it as a very pleasant tune at all.

Fast forward a few years to a different company and yet another dream about French horns. In my marketing position with this company, I spent several months working on a potential public relations partnership with a trade magazine. The program would have given my company much needed favorable publicity, but the president's resistance kept delaying a decision to move forward. Getting approval posed an uphill climb, as my boss loathed the media. I had not given up yet on trying to persuade him to change his mind, when I had this dream.

> *I was playing my horn in a group and more people began to join us. Scott [the media rep] came up behind me with a clarinet and others were standing behind. I raised my music stand so he could play along. There was a major part for the horn. I knew it well, but I couldn't get much air through the horn, so it was weak. Afterwards Scott said it was too bad and asked me if I couldn't get more air through it. I was very disappointed I couldn't.*

As much as I loathe giving up on a fantastic marketing idea, my dream offered practical advice. Despite the fact that the partnership would be an excellent opportunity to showcase our company's expertise, I could not muster enough "air" to sell it to the man in charge. Time to move on and save the fight for another day.

The orchestra analogy appears frequently, letting me know when it is time to perform. It brings greater attention to the work, the situation, or the person in the musical scenario. Practice, practice, practice is how musicians become virtuosos. My recurring dream theme reminds me when and where to focus. On the other hand, it also lets me know when I can relax a little bit and not create too much anxiety for myself.

Referring to the mystical images in dreams, "a performance" could be a significant event in one's life, an important presentation or meeting at work, or something personal like a wedding or class reunion. The latter became the subject of a dream using the recurring band theme as the messenger.

I don't think I'm the first person to think about seeing an old flame and feeling slightly anxious about it. Thoughts raced through my mind about how I looked, what I have accomplished, and whether the scene would be awkward as my old friend would see me for the first time in several years. I dreamed about my apprehensions just weeks before a milestone high school reunion.

I was doing a concert and my old boyfriend was there. During the day I saw him at a gathering, and he had a small boy with him. He talked so much, and then it was time to get ready and I had to run. I was getting dressed for the concert, then I got a few phone calls, and I looked at my watch and saw it was one minute to seven when the concert was to start. There was one person left in the band room, and I asked her to put my things away. I was on the phone and had to hang up on another person. I did not have my glasses with me and was still looking for a blouse in near panic because my horn was not out of the case and I was going to be late. I said "I gotta go" and then I woke up.

The note I wrote following this dream, scribbled while still in my sleepy haze, included two rhetorical questions: Why have I dreamed about my former boyfriend so much lately? Was I ready to see him at the reunion?

The subconscious fascinates me. Thoughts and feelings can lurk deep within the mind, and as first mentioned in my Introduction, they surface in dreams. This is what I surmised happened with my orchestra-and-boyfriend dream. It displayed all the signs of faulty preparation—missing clothing and glasses, watching the time wind down quickly, and feeling a twinge of panic. I sensed I was not ready to face my friend, yet consciously I did not give it a second thought. In fact, I didn't even know whether he would be attending the reunion.

I knew I could not ignore the dream. I looked inward and asked myself what might be causing the anxiety. Spending a few extra moments of introspection is a useful exercise, and after thinking about it I recognized a bit of guilt running through my veins. The small boy in the dream provided the clue for me. It stemmed from decades ago, when I did not treat him well during a hiatus in our youthful relationship. I determined right then and there that I would apologize to him at the reunion.

I followed through on my plan and felt an enormous sense of relief afterwards. A fine use of dream analysis put into action, I concluded.

Continuing with the musical dream theme, I have come to know that if my dream depicts me playing for an authority figure, celebrity or VIP, it is letting me know I need to rehearse before "presenting the piece." My journal contains a classic example.

The main character of my dream, Leslie, an officer of the company I worked for and one who held the purse strings, had the ability to provoke anxiety within management ranks when it came time to present our business plans. We all strived to do our best in the hope of receiving a favorable budget to get the work done. This is the dream I recorded in the midst of our planning cycle:

> *I was invited to a party at Leslie's house. I got there and introduced myself to the person who answered the door. Everybody was very formal and cold. It seemed as though I was the only person talking. I saw Leslie sitting in a chair and I said "I was looking for you." She said hello*

and went through formalities of introducing me. There would be a brass performance. I was running around and couldn't find everything. I had to run between floors of the building to get my horn and music. I told Leslie I had some pictures to show her and forgot my music. She said "tell Bob [my boss] you do not really need the music." I ran back to get stuff and I was late coming back. Everybody was warming up. I had to run and find my horn. Leslie and all the formal people were sitting and waiting for the concert. I thought about asking somebody to take a picture of the group, but I realized that nobody would want to get that personally involved and jump out to take a picture.

I would bet a year's salary that as I wrote this journal entry in 1994 I debated whether to run to my office to review the report once again, or let out a sigh of relief, feeling fully prepared and able to give the presentation "without the music." Everything turned out well, and my plan received full funding for the year.

Musicians sometimes foster reputations for being temperamental as their perfectionist tendencies for their craft spill over into other relationships. As a horn hobbyist versus a professional, I have a different perspective. When players come together in my dream scenes, it feels enormously positive. Bands or orchestras, in my opinion, represent the epitome of fine teamwork. One instrument cannot do it alone. Collaboration is a must if you want your finished work to sound pleasing to the ears. I look forward to waking up with a dream of well-tuned instruments playing together. Something must be functioning well in my life.

When I am in danger in a dream scene and suddenly a band shows up, it gives me a sense of security. I dreamed one time of being delayed in a strange airport. My plane happened to be parked near a restaurant. I went inside to check it out, and saw a crowd of clarinet and horn players, as well as flutists. My journal says it looked like a friendly place. I interpreted it to mean my destination, a customer's office, would be a welcoming place.

The trip went well, and I sold the customer new items.

If you live or work in a stressful environment, tips from any source about who is friend or foe are welcome; don't you agree?

Occasionally, a loner—or in the music world, a soloist—makes an appearance. Sometimes the musician plays beautifully and humbly accepts applause. Other times her competitive nature reveals itself, she commandeers the tempo, and the player ends up shunned by the group.

Beware the soloist in my dreams. I have learned it is a sign someone is grandstanding and may become an adversary. The sooner I can identify the good guys and the bad guys, the more comfortable I am in making decisions about where to place my trust.

I was staying at Richard's house for a band event. Everyone was having fun at the pool and Paradise Beach. Suddenly, a woman walks in, sits on the couch, and moves in. She was talking very quietly. I asked her what her name was and she said "Brullo."

She made a funny face with her lips when she said her name. She was a horn player. We had our horns out, and she took over the first chair which I was playing. She was not friendly at all. I went ahead and made something to eat and tried to ignore her. She was nasty, like a sullen teenager. Sandy [sister/advisor] was there, too, and I was saying to her how obnoxious this woman was, but I looked around and there were many band mates there so I did not want to talk about her in front of everyone. There was a knock on the door and about 20 or more band members came in. They all started hugging me and saying hi. They picked up their pool toys and went for the water. Brullo seemed to know them as they hugged her, too. I went to look for my friends, Rick and Jill, and found them on the beach. As I was running down the hill I noticed there were people buried in the sand and only their feet were sticking up. I had to dodge them to make sure I was not running over their heads. I got there and started to explain to Rick that I did not like this Brullo, and again, I realized there were many people around who might know her. I kept saying why did Richard not tell me she was coming?

I appreciate the metaphors showing up in this dream. Picture the scene. A fun group of people is living it up on Paradise Beach when an interloper crashes the party. I know there is something bad about her. (Pursed lips were a clue.) Most of the people at the party "had their heads in the sand." Her name sounded like an abrasive cleaning device. A crystal clear picture begins to emerge. My antennae go up.

You might be wondering how someone so sinister could show up as a horn player since I painted a warm picture of fellow musicians. In real life, the character depicted in this dream was not a musician at all. She ran a consulting business with questionable business ethics. She enjoyed sabotaging other people to cover up for her own mistakes, rather than acting as part of the team. Turns out she did not know the meaning of the word.

Dreams about orchestras and instruments may assert themselves into the subconscious of those who do play an instrument, but it probably loses its meaning for someone who has never performed with a group. I share my process for dissecting a dream theme to translate it into meaningful direction. I encourage you to think about examples in your own life which take on special meaning when they show themselves in your dreams. What are the metaphors inherent in your hobbies and interests?

Are you a seamstress? You may find yourself "sewing things up" in your dreams, yet it has nothing whatsoever to do with tailoring. Watch for clues in the terms you use when describing your dream. Are you "mending" anything such as a relationship?

Perhaps you enjoy hunting or fishing. Look for terminology like being "baited," or "taking a gunshot approach." Your subconscious simply uses a familiar paradigm with which you can identify and find meaning.

The mind is clever and artistic. It paints pictures so you can understand the messages being sent your way. Yet it does so in mystical ways, using metaphors. I believe it is God's way of making it memorable so I will not miss it. In fact, the funnier, the more bizarre, the better. If it happens to you, you will probably tell somebody about it, and if you are fortunate enough to have a dream buddy who helps you figure it out, the message will stick.

Some themes are more common and easier to analyze. I mentioned flying, falling and being chased as examples. Public nudity and disasters such as earthquakes and tornadoes also pop in and out of nighttime narratives. I have at least two friends who share my theme related to bridges.

Since my early childhood I dreamed a recurring scene. In fact, I could paint a picture of it still today. I am driving down a road and come to a bridge. As I drive across, water comes up and over the bridge so I am driving into the water. Frightening, no doubt.

In 1993 during a trip to my father-in-law's funeral in Indiana we came upon the same type of bridge I dreamed of dozens of times. I remember shouting, "Oh my gosh, THIS IS THE BRIDGE!" Of course, my husband had not a clue what brought on my outburst, but the picture etched itself in my mind as THE dream bridge for the next fifteen years.

If you have studied dream symbolism to any degree you know bridges in dreams are much like bridges in real life—they help you cross over to something else. It is all about transitions. Some are easier to drive over than others. Water represents emotions in dreams, so combining it with a bridge most likely represents a difficult phase in your life.

The bridges one crosses in life are many, and that is why this theme is so common. The theme started early for me, when developmental stages come quickly. As a young adult it showed up frequently in dreams as my life and career crossed one bridge after another.

I do occasionally still dream about a bridge, but the water image is gone. It did not occur to me at the time the dream theme disappeared, but the exercise of reading my journals repeatedly made me take notice.

I pinpointed the last time I had the bridge/water dream in my fortieth year. By this time I established myself in a successful career. My life seemed to be on track, and my faith in God never wavered. I cannot say my life went merrily along without further transitions, but I do believe I arrived at a point where they took less of an emotional toll.

A vexing theme repeating itself in dozens of my dreams is being late to catch an airplane. I am constantly running for a flight leaving at a specific time, with less than an hour to make it. Chaos ensues as I fuss with baggage and scramble to grab everything I need for the trip. Often I do not make the flight at all.

Most analysts agree dreaming about missing a flight may represent squandered opportunities. With each dream like this, I try to look around me to see if there is something I am missing. This is typical for me:

> *I was in a city with three other people. We had a 5:00 flight, but it was already 4:00 and we were still in a meeting. I left the meeting to find my hotel room key and was going to leave it at the desk. For*

some reason I had to take a shower, so I ran in quickly and left my clothes on. When I got my pants wet I was mad and took them off. I ran back to the room and took a laundry bag to put my wet things in. When I turned around the other people had left and went on another airline. I looked down and saw my French horn there and grabbed it. We ran to the plane and I sized it up to see if my horn would fit. The plane suddenly morphed into a bus.

It seems I am forever looking to do last-minute things like pack correctly, grab items of need, dress appropriately. Experts pose varying opinions on why someone dreams in this theme. Reasons vary from a tendency to procrastinate to a propensity to sabotage one's own progress.

I have given it serious thought and determined this is my perfectionism manifesting itself in dreams. I arrived at my conclusion by combining all the other recurring themes with the flight theme, and it makes sense. If perfection is the overriding goal, opportunities will be missed. Each time I have a dream similar to the one above, I look in the mirror to see whether I am holding myself back. Denise, a friend and a mentor, has a favorite saying: "Perfect is stupid." I get it.

7

BODY SENSE

It amazes me how millions of Americans are out of touch with their bodies. Many do not realize something is physically wrong until it grows to crisis proportions. Having a home-based business in the wellness industry, I have seen this time and again. I meet dozens of people who had no idea their bodies harbored cancer, for example, until it manifested itself in such a significant way they needed intense and immediate treatment.

The Gynecologic Cancer Foundation did a study in 2010 of women 19-25 years of age to find out how much they knew about the cervix. Only 17% of these women even knew what their cervix did. Twice as many women surveyed knew more about the hottest music than they did about how to maintain a healthy reproductive system.

Public service announcements explain how to spot signs of cancer, yet many people have no idea it is growing in their bodies until it is too late. Doesn't it sound like a good idea to rely on another source—your "gutometer"—to help you identify when something is amiss?

My dreams have acted like a doting grandmother by letting me know where to look when I am under the weather. "You probably have a cold coming on," Gram would say to me when she noticed my energy level waning.

Cyndi Dale is an intuitive counselor who often receives referrals from psychiatrists, medical doctors and therapists to assist in finding the source of problems in their patients. Cyndi founded The Energy Medicine program, taught at Normandale College in Bloomington, Minnesota. It is based on her award-winning and top-selling book, *The Subtle Body: An Encyclopedia of Your Energetic Anatomy.*

Energy medicine is a fast growing profession. Knowing what Cyndi does in this field, and having witnessed her abilities, convinces me the body sends out signals on a regular basis. I believe dreams are one way to tap into the source. If you listen carefully to their message, you will uncover clues about things going on in your body.

I have honed my intuitive skills utilizing my dream journals to stay on top of my own health. There have been times when I knew without a doubt my body had something going on physically. I may not always be able to put my finger on it, and it may not be to the point where I can explain it to a doctor. I just know.

I am fortunate to have good health today, but I went through some difficult times in the past when physical ailments played a prominent role. There have been times doctors could not find the problem without a battery of tests, but I knew where to look.

An especially vivid dream confirmed for me the source of abdominal pain I suffered through for months. Apologies for graphic detail aside, I wholeheartedly encourage you to write specifically, as I did, when describing physical images appearing in your dreams.

> My dream: *I was chased by a woman named Kansak who was trying to kill me. I hid in cars. Each time I saw her she was in striped overalls hunting me down. I looked down to my chest and saw there was a hole forming. I*

could see inside my esophagus and the little thing in back of my throat. I could even see pretzels and other food in there. I took my friend, Deanna, aside and asked her what to do, and she said I must see a specialist. But it was a weekend and I did not think anyone would be there. She said not to eat anything until Monday. Then I asked [my friend] Gary to have a look at it and he was flabbergasted. He said I should go immediately.

From the description in my journal, I suspected the pain had something to do with my digestive system. Beyond that, I surmised it was due to work related stress. The would-be killer in the dream, Kansak, is a brand name for a product we sold at the time. Metaphorically speaking, my job was "killing me."

It is true at the time the dream occurred, a stressful dynamic played out between people working in my department. It affected all of us, and for me, it took its toll physically. Deanna and Gary, both friends and co-workers who understood the circumstances, played advisory roles in the dream and in real life.

I did my research on stress-related health issues and narrowed it down to two possible issues. At the doctor's appointment I offered up my theories, and she said she would test for them both. The physician eventually zeroed in on one of them—acid reflux—and I felt a sense of relief for that versus something more serious. We put a treatment plan in place, and within a few months I felt immensely better.

A disclaimer is necessary at this point. I would never suggest you substitute dreams for a professional medical opinion. My approach to using the dream, however, did make the detective work easier. In a ten-minute appointment, a doctor may use up the entire time asking questions, trying to pinpoint your issues and still have to send you for a myriad of tests to determine the cause. Since my intuition told me the source of my issues, I guided the doctor's line of questioning and achieved results in a shorter time.

Most people agree that today's lifestyles contribute to our own health issues. We know we have to lose weight, exercise more, sleep better, quit smoking, and on and on. Spouses, family members, and friends become thorns in our side when they try to help by reminding us of all we need to be doing to stay well. We have learned our habits do not change until it is our own idea. Quitting smoking, for example, does not usually happen simply because your spouse requested you to do so.

Doesn't it make sense, then, to use your subconscious as a wellness coach? It represents your own deepest thoughts, not those of a well-meaning, but nagging friend. If the idea of eating right or taking a brisk walk comes from within, you may be more apt to do it. It worked for me, inciting me to join a yoga class, after I had an alarming dream about my physical state.

I was in a bar looking around and pointing out people from the foodservice industry who had been around for years. Everybody wanted to go out and eat, but I needed a shower. I kept saying I would do that, and then I would run into somebody else I had to talk to. Then I took time to fill out a comment card and looked for a place to put it. I ended up taping it to the door of a cabinet where a housekeeper would find it. Finally, somebody said it was 9 o'clock and restaurants would be closing so I said ok, let's go. There was an x-ray machine we had to walk through on our way in. I was surprised at how my bones looked. It seemed that my back was out of alignment, and I remember thinking that I needed to get in shape physically.

The story in this dream establishes a fact. I worked in the foodservice industry for many years, and eating out in restaurants is a way of life. Perhaps the shower image says I tried to "get clean" and opt out of the restaurant experience. Notice the procrastination attempts I made until finally relenting and heading for the restaurant. The x-ray machine I saw as a wake-up call to do something to improve myself physically.

I joined a yoga class, a challenge for me, as the class met in the middle of my work day. Workaholics like me rarely do things like this for ourselves if it means missing an hour at the desk. It turned out to be one of the best moves for me. My physical strength improved, and most importantly, the class did wonders for stress relief. It took a visual of deteriorating bones to get me to do it, and I thank my dream guides for putting it up on the screen for me.

Another body related dream left me with more questions than answers until I pieced it together with lab tests and had my "aha" moment. I had pain and cramping which I felt related to a female issue. This dream image may be a creepy way of describing a physical situation, but the stirring visual helps put the medical issue in terms I can understand.

Last night I dreamed that I was in the hospital with pains in my abdomen. While I was on the bed all the nurses were watching TV and eating junk food and throwing the garbage on my bed. At first they decided my back was the problem so they put a pillow under my legs. After they thought it was my back they decided it might be something else so they said they had to snip my ovary! They went in there with some antiseptic to clean it, stuck a long handled scissors in and snipped. Blood and fluid splattered all over the place and all the nurses scattered and left. They stuffed Kleenex up there to soak it up. Suddenly a guy drove up in a small yellow car, like a Yugo, and said to get in it and he would take me home. When he looked at the table I was on, some leftover chicken, snack food and garbage were under the sheets.

Searching the Internet and my medical encyclopedia, I looked for ailments described in terms of debris taking up residence in the body. Sure enough, I found it. Endometriosis is a condition where cells and tissue end up in places they should not be. Another related malady is fibroids, which are unusual growths in the uterine wall. Hence, the food and garbage image in the dream. Lab tests confirmed both.

After some head scratching, I perceived the Yugo reference to be emblematic as well. Notice the car is yellow, and if you remember my discussion of colors in Chapter 3, yellow can be an indication of sickness.

The first word I would use to describe a Yugo is "cheap." Why would I find a reference to frugality in a body-related dream? Proving my point, you sometimes have to stick with it to figure out obscure references in your dreams. They do not always present themselves with great clarity.

It took me some time to arrive at a reasonable interpretation. Doctors gave me two options for treatment of the conditions—a hysterectomy or a uterine fibroid embolization. I chose the latter, a minimally invasive and *less expensive* technique.

8

TRANSITIONS

The inability to cope with change will provide subject matter for writers, business leaders, psychologists, intuitive counselors, and life coaches for decades to come. Some people pretend to like change and then fight it every step of the way. Politicians promote their promises of change in every election. Yet many people just do not deal well with it emotionally.

My dreams are full of imagery depicting significant changes in my life, and I put them to good use in managing transition. Dreams alert me to emotional blockades I inadvertently create in resistance to change, and they prepare me when transition is inevitable.

A scene comes into my dreams repeatedly in which I am packing, unpacking, and moving offices. My real life world provided enough action to create a metaphor warehouse. Four company mergers in a five-year period, personnel rotations within my work group, and my own job changes and promotions created rich material to keep me dreaming indefinitely. In fact, I could have added Office Relocation to Chapter 6, Dream Themes. It happened so often, the pages in one of my favorite books, *Who Moved My Cheese?*, are dog-eared.

My wish for you is to utilize the examples from my dream journals to devise a method of your own to manage life's transitions. Here's a classic example of mine:

> *I went into my office and found a guy sitting there with his stuff out on the desk. There was also a large file cabinet, so it was very crowded. As we talked, it became apparent that he was the new director who was just hired. And he had taken over the place. I kind of let him do it, and I moved to a different cube and started opening drawers to move in. It was filthy! Old glasses in the drawers and many of the drawers did not work. I started cleaning it when I said to myself how unfair this was. He had even taken down the pictures on my walls. I went to find the*

woman in charge and told her what happened. She said he was supposed to have an office already set aside, that he did not need mine. I also told her it was unfair that they had given me a cube rather than an office, and it was in the middle of a department I did not know. She went to find out what was happening. I was anxious and couldn't wait so I followed her there. She was in his office and they had 19 people squeezed in like they were having a party. I stood outside and counted them, hoping she was going to come out and tell me to move back into my office.

The same night I continued dreaming—a double header with a similar transition theme.

I went from the office to an airport where we were having a meeting. The rooms were large dorm-like rooms. Some had several beds in them and others just had one. I found the first one and grabbed a double bed. Many others were twins. I put my stuff in the drawers of the dresser. I must have gone off to something else, and when I came back somebody else had moved in. I was trying to find the original room I was in, and somebody was in each room where I looked. In one room there were two twin beds. There was a guy unpacking, so I knew that wasn't mine. Several times I looked into a dresser drawer to see if it was my stuff; the drawer was full of jewelry and personal items. Finally I went back to what I thought was the first room. I walked past an area where everybody was eating. It was a country-western barbecue and they were frying up huge steaks. I saw a lot of people from work, and so I kept walking. I never did find the right room.

If this were one of my first attempts at interpreting a dream, I would say the story is obvious. Intimidation from a new person coming aboard may create fear of him replacing me. The second dream might have been a metaphor for trying to find where I belonged. The barbecue image depicted everyone having fun, oblivious to the transition looming before me.

This is why I suggest taking your time and putting the images into context rather than rushing to a conclusion. In reality, I welcomed the man named in my dream as a solid addition to the team. (I left his name out, as I do not want any misunderstandings because I dreamed about him. He is a good guy.) I harbored no ill will toward him whatsoever. This dream could have been about him, or someone in a similar position. It might also be referring to someone with his qualities. Some experts would say the character might actually be referring to me.

The journal entry above could have more than one meaning. There were other changes going on in my life at the same time. It happened to come during a period of personal transition. My husband and I were considering moving, and unbeknownst to anyone but me, I started thinking about life as if I were living alone. The twin beds in the second scene provided the clue that I finally admitted this to myself. My deepest thoughts were beginning to bubble up, creeping into my dreams before they were ever uttered out loud. The images clearly depicted a person who didn't know where she belonged at the moment.

Relationships are often at the center of painful transitions, whether personal or professional. At one point in my career I replaced a colleague, Matt, in his position after he left for another company. Matt and I worked closely together, so I knew much about his job. I observed how he handled clients and became a student of his style. His method lined up diametrically opposite from mine, but I appreciated how he approached the business. I saw what worked and what did not. From an intellectual standpoint, the transition into his job went along seamlessly.

Emotionally, however, it turned into a bumpy ride.

After so many months of traveling and working together, I considered Matt a friend as well as a colleague. I confided in him on work issues, and our individual outlooks on the company's direction were basically the same.

Strategic alignment and execution are critical pieces to success. Matt and I saw eye to eye strategically, but my way of getting the job done differed substantially.

Matt left the company, but we still had occasions to meet socially, since Matt and another friend, Barry, and I were like "the three musketeers." A few weeks after the transition, I sensed Matt avoiding me. Not sure whether it stemmed from my imagination or reality, I asked Barry to play the role of go-between, with minimal success.

What should have been a happy time for me, with a promotion and new-job euphoria, rather disturbed me because of an apparent rift it caused in our friendship. I did not know why Matt avoided me, and my feelings were hurt.

Barry and I discussed it.

Could it be because I changed a few programs Matt implemented? Did he regret leaving because of negative vibes in his new job? I already established strong relationships with Matt's former customers. Did he feel as if he was not missed?

It bothered me so much it started to show up at night in a series of dreams.

I dreamed I had a plan to burn down my office building. I lit a fire and thought I would have time to get things out. I grabbed a few things and threw them outside. I went to the closet and grabbed a couple of winter coats. I tried to go back for photo albums, but it was too hot. Suddenly I realized the fire was out of control, and I had to get out. Investigators asked me questions, and I was evasive, covering something up, and asking some of my closest friends to do the same. The rest of the dream dealt with getting the office rebuilt. I felt I wanted to start over with fresh things, but I was stupid enough to think I could get away with this. I remembered thinking how dumb I was that I did not have a better plan for getting things out of the building.

Fires in dreams can be a sign of transformation. Just as they do in waking life, fires cleanse the forest of rotting wood and bring new growth. Metaphorically, the scenario may have been sending me a message about saving the most meaningful things in "my house" while letting the old, unimportant things go.

My friendship with Matt was important to me. I admonished myself for somehow being responsible for the strained relationship with him. Yet, I couldn't place my finger on what I may have done.

Reinforcement of this painful transition came four nights later when the fire theme repeated itself in this dream:

> *I was on a ship, watching crew members in the elevators and noticed the floor was getting hot. They were discussing getting lifeboats out, but they weren't calling for an alarm yet. I saw a guy I recognized from years ago; he was going to be a guest speaker. It was a training session, and I was going to introduce him. Lots of people were coming in to hear him speak. I told him that*

whenever he was ready, to go ahead and start; in the meantime I ran around looking for the fire. Another guy and I took the mics and engaged in witty banter. I was thinking we should sing Amazing Grace, but he came up with something else. He said I should be tired because of all the stuff going on, but I brushed it aside and said it was so much fun it did not matter.

I believe Matt is the guest speaker, the trainer. It made sense to me since Matt recently spent days training me to take over his job. I knew Barry and I handled the microphones, because "witty banter" is a hallmark of our relationship, as we joked to lighten up a serious office mood.

Rather than admonishing myself, as I did in the first dream, for not having a better plan to preserve things in the old building, I decided to let the fire burn. It signified moving forward for me. For regrowth to flourish, I had to stop beating myself up over the erosion of the friendship and plunge forward with my plans in the new position. The second dream seemed to evolve from the first and point to a suggested path for me to take. Get back to the *witty banter* and stop worrying about the fire.

It turns out I made the right decision to move on, as I enjoyed success and strengthened my background for the next opportunity. It brought me little satisfaction emotionally, as my relationship with Matt continued to be nonexistent. Fortunately, about a year later, I bumped into him on an airplane, and a friendly discussion took place. I never did find out what changed the relationship in his mind. Perhaps that will show up in a dream yet to come.

Transitions in relationships take a toll emotionally, while the shifts made in a career or lifestyle are more mentally taxing for me. Relocating to a new place can lead to a depressing feeling because the local support structure is gone. Of course, true friends and loving family will stand by you no matter how far away they are, but the urge to chat with a neighbor or have coffee with a friend remains. The void left from a significant move is palpable.

Combine more than one transition, and the feeling of not belonging anywhere can overwhelm even the strongest will. I experienced this when I left the corporate work world, ended a marriage, and moved to a new state all within a year. Outwardly I tried to show my ability to juggle all the balls with aplomb. My insecurities stayed below the surface until the middle of the night. During the first year of my life transition, unsettling dreams like this one were common:

Dreamed all night about WFF [the women's organization mentioned previously.] I was not fitting in anywhere at the conference. I was there early, got a seat and ran into Karen [an old friend.] I invited her to sit by us, but she went somewhere else. Later I had to leave for a bit, and when I came back the room was full, and everyone was in a breakout session. I couldn't figure out where to go. I had no materials with me and did not have a table assignment. I went to find some lunch, and there was nothing to eat. Even the snack bar was empty.

I could have skipped through the analytics of this dream and just wallowed in self pity for a few days, as it clearly depicted a sad situation. Woe is me, I don't seem to belong anywhere in this dream. In fact, the depression loomed so large I woke up and considered going right back to sleep to shake it.

Instead, I forced myself to read through the journal entry with a different lens. Why did I have such a sense of loss attending the conference in the dream? I am a charter member of the WFF, a former Board director, and a participant in at least fifteen annual conferences. I knew the ropes. Friends and I enjoyed a wonderful time every year.

I reflected on what changed since the last time I attended the conference in real life. I now ran my own company. I no longer shared the same cause—advancing a corporate career—with the other members. Once I looked at it in a new light and realized it not as a loss, just a transition, I celebrated the progress I made as well as that of the organization.

My work life had undergone a radical change. The transition dreams did not stop, but they followed a progression of sorts. The setting of my dreams shifted. Rather than placing my stories in a corporate office, I subconsciously dreamed in new locations and even created new metaphors to reflect a changing lifestyle.

I took on a new home-based business in addition to my consulting work. Not an intentional career move on my part, I believe The Universe meant for me to take it on. It came about after serious health crises turned everything upside down for both my friend—now my life partner—and me within a one-year period. We became users of, and eventually distributors for, a health supplement drink. The unfamiliar science behind it created a need to explain it to people in some detail. Human nature being what it is, the people who first heard about it deemed it too good to be true, so the early adopters, including us, spent a lot of time developing believers through education.

The paradigm shift is immense. Consulting in an industry I know well is turnkey. Learning a new industry takes hard work as the focus turns to a new audience. Not everyone jumps at the chance to learn about emerging science. Some come from the camp of "if I have not heard of it on television, it can't be true." Others, still reeling from recessionary losses in personal wealth, fear they cannot afford it. It is a constant internal conflict, as I immediately want to give it away to people desperately looking for help, yet I know its value will be lost on someone who does not buy it—or buy into it—in the first place. The struggle manifested itself in this dream:

> *I dreamed I was in a church and lots of people were there. ASEA [the health supplement] reps were in front. I had a hard time getting from the balcony to the front of the church. There were many levels and stairs. I opened one door and found water right there. I walked up some stairs and a guy was behind bars. He reached out and grabbed my ankle. Another guy with a large spear threw it at my car. I said to myself, "this is a scary place, I have to get out." One*

of the ASEA guys asked me to handle the equipment—head phones and microphones—but I couldn't figure them out. I dumped them on a counter. I looked in another room, and it had a bed in it suggesting people spent the night there. One guy took pity on me and started talking. I was going to tell him about all the bad things going on, but we were interrupted.

Where should I begin with this analysis? Each sentence reveals an emotion or thought building up inside me for months.

Let's start with the church full of people. It represents the believers—people like me who experienced firsthand the power of the product and became "evangelists" for the company.

Going from the balcony, or the cheap seats, to the front of the church requires navigating levels and obstacles. From water to creepy guys, to weapons—this dream has its share of them. The supplement is a specially formulated water, so this image had double meaning. The dream guides threw one challenge after another in front of me. Frustrated from trying to figure out how to use the equipment in the scene, I gave up.

In the dream I could see people devoted a lot of time to this endeavor—so much so that they *spent the night there.* It reflects real life accurately. People sacrifice personal time and interests to take the news to the marketplace. The *guy behind bars* reached out for help, grabbing my ankle. To me he represented people desperately seeking an answer to a troublesome health issue.

Any "normal" person might look at the obstacle course depicted and decide it is not for her. In fact, the dream insinuates an uphill climb by inserting the poor guy who *took pity on me.* Just about the time the dream seems to be telling me to chuck it all, a subliminal message appears. *I was going to tell him about all the bad things going on, but we got interrupted.* No time for dwelling on the negatives. The story does not allow for that; so it's time to charge forward.

I watch for signs in a dream of a life transition causing too much stress. According to dream dictionaries, classic sleep symbols of stress include death, storms, crashes, or references to hell. Fortunately, I do not have many of those to report. A more common stress image is the loss of teeth, which may signify insecurity or embarrassment, even helplessness. I do have a tooth drama to share.

> My dream: *I dreamed a company was having a big barbecue. I said I had to leave to pick up Ray at 3:00. It was only 1:30. I pulled my car up to the barbecue area and I was going to wait for the right time. I took out a piece of gum and as I was chewing I felt something hard in it. I reached in and found that I had lost a tooth – the eye tooth. I thought to myself, I wonder why I am losing so many teeth lately? I went up to the picnic area, and I had to get permission to leave with things in my hand. I went to a person that looked like the company secretary and opened my hand. In it I had a bunch of thumbtacks and the tooth. I said I was leaving and taking these with me. She reached*

in and said she could use some of these and grabbed a tack. I left with my tooth.

This dream occurred shortly after I left my last corporate position to go out on my own. I did not let it concern me too much because I assumed any entrepreneur has her moments when she questions whether she did the right thing in leaving a secure job. The good omen in this dream is that I did leave *with my tooth*, an indication to me that if I have any underlying insecurities, I possess the ability to get over them.

There are two other indications of distress I occasionally find peeking out from under the covers. One of them is finding myself publicly naked or caught in the bathroom. They have similar meanings according to experts.

Dream expert, Tony Crisp, explains that discovering yourself nude in a dream may point to vulnerability, inferiority, or exposure you may be feeling. Being caught in the bathroom usually indicates there is an issue of which you need to "relieve yourself." Being caught in a public bathroom without stalls or walls of protection ranks the symbolism higher on the stress chart. It has a dual meaning. It may signify you are putting others' needs ahead of your own, which leads to a sense of losing personal space.

"Alternatively," says *Dream Moods*, "the dream indicates that you are having difficulties letting go of old emotions. You are afraid that if you reveal these feelings, then others around you will judge and criticize you."

I felt especially vulnerable when my employer of sixteen years decided to merge the company with our largest competitor, and I uncovered numerous naked or bathroom based nightmares in my journal during the integration period. This is just one of many I dreamed during the eighteen months it took to complete the acquisition. Many of them revealed insecurities because of fear of the unknown.

> My dream: *Dreamed I had been arrested or detained at a police station and I was trying to leave but couldn't find my way out. I went out to the garage from the station and there were some*

creepy gang members there who started following me so I turned around and went back into the station. I asked at the counter if there was a police officer who could drive me to a cabstand or all the way home. A person at the counter said there was not anybody available. I started crying and said there were creepy guys out there. The cop said she would look for somebody and come and get me if she found someone. So I waited inside. I went to the bathroom and there were no doors on the stalls, so I was sitting there tinkling and a great big guy came in and started going right next to me. I was afraid he would come over and attack me while I was going. I finished and looked into another room and saw Blair[co-worker]there filling out paperwork. I was so embarrassed and did not want him to see me so I ducked out. I went back to the counter to ask if they had found someone to give me a ride. The cop said they had someone who was looking for me, but when they couldn't find me he had to go on to another case. I went to the back again and tried to walk around the building, to avoid the gang members. I never did make my way out of the police station before I woke up.

I knew at once this related to the merger because Blair, a friend formerly employed by my company, now worked for the competitor we were acquiring. The "creepy guys" were probably any of those involved in compiling the list of those who would get laid off. My gut, reinforced by my "gut-ometer," told me it would not be a happy place to work for the foreseeable future. Shortly thereafter I decided this would not be a desirable place to work.

Transitions can be healthy when they open up opportunity for growth, but repeated images of stress in dreams should wake you up and wave a giant red flag. Learning to manage stress or finding a solid foundation in some other area of your life will hopefully turn these dreams into happier scenes. I decided to be proactive about my future and agreed to interview with another company.

Not all transition dreams leave one feeling lost or out of control. Look for welcoming images, such as friends who show up at the moment when needed. One such dream features my pastor and Steve, a friend from church, driving, with me in his car. They saved me from myself.

> My dream: *We drove along a beach and sank into the sand watching a parade of boats. It seemed to be in a foreign country, maybe Mexico. We made it through the sand and then found ourselves flying over a ravine in a little car. I moved forward in my seat and suddenly felt the urge to jump out before we got across the ravine. I caught myself at the last minute and we made it across. Pastor Peter looked at me and was about to ask me what I was doing. I said "Phew, I almost jumped out but held myself back." He patted my hand. I looked at the back of Steve's sweater and there were*

two little pockets with Kleenex in them. I pulled them out. He said he knew they were there for me, and he was glad I took them.

I give people, like my pastor, who grace my dreams frequently offering aid and comfort, a special designation. I call them my "advisors" and share more about their role in Chapter 13 Advisory Board. I also feel good when restful places such as churches or resorts appear in dreams because they connote a feeling of relaxation or peace. Unfortunately, these do not show up often in transition dreams.

Many co-workers and friends I have known over the past thirty years have labored over crucial decisions affecting their careers. Even though their transitions did not necessarily affect me personally, I empathized so much with their situation that they showed up in my dreams.

It does not matter if the person is an ambitious corporate executive, or someone who works to put food on the table without regard for the corporation's success. Decisions about making a job change, especially if it includes moving the family, can create high anxiety and put stress on relationships. I feel everyone's pain, so I dream about them.

Jerry, a close friend and co-worker, agonized over making a decision to move to Los Angeles from the Midwest to take the next step up in his sales career. Uprooting three kids and his wife from their comfortable suburban lifestyle to climb the corporate ladder is a decision fraught with drama and sleepless nights.

Many of my colleagues and I were forced to make similar decisions, for better or worse. Some marriages barely survived such turmoil, while a few families enjoyed greener pastures in their new home town. More often than not, the budding executive did his time and quickly loaded up the truck to return home at the earliest opportunity.

Jerry made a decision that would come to shorten his tenure at our company. He confided in me during negotiations, and I based my advice partly on this dream:

Dreamed that I was teaching
classes about dreams and what
they meant and how to interpret

them. Jerry was deciding which class he wanted to teach. There were 3 classes to choose from— history, economics and political science. Each one was a disaster, kids running all around, and no organization. I would run back and forth between the rooms to help him decide which one to go with. I got tied up and ran back to Jerry's room late, and he was panicky because he didn't know what to say or do. He had the students start telling each other about dreams.

I believe the three classes referred to the factors Jerry needed to weigh in his decision of whether or not to accept the promotion. The history of the position and the territory he would be taking over could come into play. The previous salesperson, well respected in the market, announced his retirement. He planned to stay on as a consultant in a part-time role, but he would not be face to face with customers on a regular basis. He had been there a long time and established solid relationships. It could be an advantage because the territory ran well, with few issues, or it might be a challenge trying to live up to the reputation the previous representative established.

The economics class mentioned in the dream refers to the obvious financial factors Jerry would need to consider in his decision to move. The cost of living in California ranked as one of the highest in the country. Transportation costs were at a premium to his current expenses.

The third class—political science—depicted a potential landmine, as politics always come into play in companies as job transitions occur. There would be a load of politics to deal with no matter which way Jerry decided to go.

The chaotic scene provided no obvious solution to Jerry's dilemma. None of the areas jumped out as the overriding factor in his decision. One area did feel familiar to me—it related to dreams. Just as I am suggesting in this book, the dream told me Jerry needed to make a decision based on what his gut told him to do, politics be damned.

9

PREMONITIONS

Have you ever experienced an alarming dream about someone and felt the urge to call and make sure they were alright? I have done it dozens of times, sometimes confessing the specifics of the premonition dream to my leading lady or gentleman and enjoying a chuckle or two.

Other times, when I dream about something particularly disturbing, such as a death, I pick up the phone and call the "deceased" just to be sure a live human answers. All kind of silly, as I now know, having studied dream analysis. A dream death is not necessarily predicting it for the person himself, rather a characteristic or aspect of life he represents. It might also signify something within you that "died."

Experts say premonitions may come from dreams if the subject is something that can really happen. Others in the scientific community claim we do not have enough information yet to understand whether premonition dreams are possible.

Dr. Keith Hearne, PhD, founder of the European College of Hypnotherapy, lays out his theory, claiming the jury is still out on whether premonitions through dreams are a possibility. There are plenty of accounts of people who saw an event in a dream before it occurred. I will leave it up to you to choose your side of this argument.

Anecdotally, there are dramatic examples of premonitions which lead the dreamer to take a course of action, averting tragedy. There are stories of would-be passengers of the Titanic which claim dreams actually saved lives. Mrs. Esther Hart, it's been told, dreamed of impending doom for the ship. Since her vision saw the ship go down in the middle of the night, she reportedly slept during the day as if to ward off the nighttime doom she feared. (Mrs. Hart and her seven-year old daughter survived the tragic voyage.) A second passenger dreamed of a stranger standing near her who asked if she loved life and suggested she get off at the next port.

I feel it is important to pay attention to such dreams simply because they are disturbing and may uncover other issues. My philosophy is there's no harm in checking on someone if you think you "saw" a looming disaster in nightmare form.

Over the years of my own journaling, I noted curious dreams I would categorize as predictive. Practically speaking, they were helpful in problem solving more than alarming. One dream rated high on my gut gauge because it confirmed a nagging suspicion I harbored regarding an employee.

> My dream: *I went to a house where I was supposed to meet Sylvia Brown, a psychic. I couldn't find her in the lower level, so I started to go upstairs when I heard a noise. Three kids looked over the railing and asked me if I was looking for Tony [an employee.] I asked them why, was he there? Yes, they said; he was in the den. I entered a small office, and Tony was in a rocking chair with his iPod on, eyes closed listening to something. His*

computer was on the desk. I poked him awake, and he scrambled to turn his computer off so I wouldn't see what was on his screen.

Tony, an outstanding employee, had been on my mind for weeks before this dream occurred. I had a feeling he considered leaving the company. This dream seemed to reinforce my gut feel about his intentions, so I focused on doing what I could to make sure he received support and encouragement to continue doing a great job. Yet I knew I would soon lose him. Sure enough, he resigned a few weeks later.

The dream helped me from a practical standpoint because it kicked me into planning mode. Typically a surprise two-week resignation notice results in one of these things happening—all undesirable for office efficacy. Often the position stays open and co-workers cover the best they can, with many projects getting lost in the transition. Other times business suffers as customers experience a void of coverage while the company service staff runs around figuring out what to do. Another option is for the boss to step in and cover the post. Depending upon how well versed he is in the details of the job, he frequently makes matters worse.

My preference is to know the person is leaving well before the two-week lame duck period and have time to develop a sound, well-thought-out plan to replace the employee. Several weeks' "early notice" on Tony because of my dream intuition gave me the time I needed to create a succession plan and lay the foundation for it to occur quickly and successfully when he actually resigned.

I have seen night visions of strange, distressful and wonderful things happening to friends. I could call them plain old intuition, but when they turned out to accurately predict events, who can question whether it isn't some kind of premonition?

Liz and I were co-workers and friends living a parallel path in our personal and professional lives. We both married men with children from previous marriages, so step kids were a frequent topic of conversation. We shared the challenges of working in a male dominated work environment, such as the strains that can burden a marriage. It stood to reason she and I occasionally discussed the topic of divorce. I wondered if it loomed on the horizon for either of us. This dream told me, for her, she already reached a decision.

Dreamed that Liz's husband, Mark, had been convicted of something and was sentenced to death. The dream centered around all of us from work gathering in a place to watch, and we did not know whether he would get a reprieve or not. We called a medical center person and asked where the event was taking place and were told to go to a certain building and room. All of us were huddling outside the auditorium. Liz and others were inside waiting for the verdict. They did a drum roll and then they said Mark will.........not have to die. Everyone cheered but Liz just sat there, stone faced. Her grandma and mom were there but were oblivious to what was happening. We all hugged Mark, but Liz just stood there. I couldn't even remember what his crime was.

A few months later, the "verdict" came in. They were divorced.

I adore premonition dreams that allow a peek at something fabulous happening in the future. I appreciated one during a tumultuous time at work, making it even sweeter. Uncertainty clouded the environment while my employer dealt with an acquisition, and I interviewed with another company just shortly after the tragic events of 9/11/2001.

For weeks I suffered with gloomy, unnerving dreams which probably put me with the majority of Americans during an uncertain time for our country. I had no clue when, or if, the merger would close, and as a result, I did not know whether I would get the new job as it hinged on government approval and agreement by the parties. I welcomed the following dream as a good omen, not knowing it would be only ten days until the announcement that these two giants in the food business would become one.

My dream: *I was going on a business trip and Gloria [my administrative assistant] brought me my papers. It was a cruise. She said the only difference between this and the last cruise I had taken is I would be in a first-class cabin on the upper level. A guy standing nearby said this trip would be very windy, and I would probably get sick from the motion back and forth. I boarded the cruise, and almost immediately they took us to an undisclosed island for a special side trip. They said it was for security reasons. On the beach there were black submarines buried in the sand like it was from a war. I went back to the ship and walked into the library. A guy in there told me this was Leek's Island.*

Wow! Not only did this dream predict I would be upgraded to first class (the new job), but it suggested there would be collateral damage along the way. Wind-in-dream symbolism is almost always a sign of significant change in the air.

Looking further you will find a library reference. In dreams, libraries symbolize learning or information. You might have missed the hint as to where the information came from, as I did at first, because of my nighttime spelling. Leek's Island could also be Leak's Island.

The submarine remnants of war painted a vivid picture of many months of unpleasant integration activities as the two fierce competitors engaged in the business of putting the companies together. There were plenty of landmines. The dream accurately predicted a tense and difficult environment which carried over once the acquisition was wrapped up.

There were times I clearly felt a premonition in my sleep, and one had a seismic impact. For several years I owned a home in California, not far from the San Andreas fault. Our community hosted earthquake preparedness training, and we were always well rehearsed for the next "big one." One sleepy night I dreamed:

> *Carla and I were walking around campus reminiscing. We saw Jeff working at a table handing out copies of magazines. He asked for my ID as Carla and I turned to walk into the library. While we*

were there, we had a huge earthquake, and everyone got down on the floor. Books came tumbling off the shelves along with a little wooden box I have had for years and where I kept my treasures as a kid. I opened it up, and some little stones were in it, and I realized it was not mine and put it back on the shelf.

I awoke to the news that at 4:56 a.m. there had indeed been a 4.7 magnitude earthquake centered about seven miles from my home. The *little wooden box* reminded me I might not be as organized as I thought. I owned a wooden box which contained some valuable items that I should have put into the safety deposit box. I did so the very next day.

The reason why I tend to believe premonition dreams do occur is that I see the evidence right there in my journal. There it is in black and white. Some predictions manifested quickly, such as the earthquake dream, and others left my consciousness as soon as I wrote them down. If you keep journals for any length of time, you will find it fascinating to go back and read them with the benefit of hindsight. You, too, might be convinced there is a predictive element to your dreams.

One of the benefits in writing this book is reminding myself of the mystery and magic of dreams. When you know the real-life outcome of a story born in a dream, you may want to share the details, especially of those with captivating plots.

Two of my dreams, both eerily accurate, occurred a month apart and two-and-a-half years before the plot line became an actual drama. It had to do with a customer indicted in a securities fraud scheme.

My journal entries read like excerpts from a dime-store novel. Collateral damage of the main event consisted of indictments of several suppliers involved, including someone who worked at a company we were acquiring. He would have worked in my department if I stayed with that company. Public records show, unbeknownst to any of us at the acquiring company, the activities in question were apparently taking place at the time I had this dream. The customer's executives were arrested and convicted.

The first dream concerned the vice president of purchasing. I'll call him Ted in this excerpt.

Dreamed Ted invited me over, and he was driving a vehicle that was a renovated fire truck. It was huge. He lived in an old house, a dirty old bachelor pad. I excused myself to go to the bathroom. When I came back he was on the floor looking as if he was having a seizure, red faced, sweaty, and falling over. He looked as if he was on drugs or drunk. He had thrown up. I tried to pick him up, but he was too big. I got him up with Sandy's help [my sister/advisor.] I got in the car and tried to drive. It was challenging. He was sloppy drunk and hugged me. He said he always liked me. I finally got him to the airport.

Ted is one of those customers you love to hate. His company represented a lot of potential business, but he treated suppliers with disdain. I never looked forward to meeting with him. The dirty bachelor pad image reinforced my opinion of him as a seedy character.

A second dream transmitted itself like the next episode in a television series.

I had just taken an important job and found out somebody who was working for me would be arrested. It was a guy, and though his name was not mentioned, his image looked like someone I know. It had something to do with work, but I never found out what he did. I was invited to a company outing, and we were fishing and doing leisure activities. It started raining, and I asked my friend Jim what he was going to do. He said he would fish in the rain. I decided to stay inside and all sorts of people were around. I asked if I should wear gloves so I wouldn't ruin any fingerprints of the people getting arrested. I looked outside and there were dozens of police officers waiting to take this person into custody. The whole dream centered on my trying to help convict this person by finding evidence.

There is no denying my dream foretold an actual event involving a distributor and implicating several suppliers at the same time. Court records showed the crimes for which these people were convicted happened in fiscal year 2001. I recorded this dream on December 2, 2001. It would be July of 2004 before the Securities and Exchange Commission pressed charges, and two years later the first convictions were publicized. Premonition?

One lesson I have learned from reading my journals repeatedly is if you cannot pinpoint a current situation from the dream's messages, ask yourself whether it might be a premonition dream. I wish I had done it more thoughtfully, as I may have saved myself some aggravation, if not surprise, later on. This is one dream I put on the list of those to which "I wish I would have paid heed."

Dreamed people were trying to break into our house. Two women in a car came up to the house, and as I was lowering the garage door, they jumped in. I had to beat them off with a broom. I kept telling Tom [husband] we needed to do something about it, but he pretty much ignored me. The next time I saw someone coming by the house I tried to get the car's license number. Tom wrote it down. I called 911 and a woman told me I had the wrong address. When the screen came up it had someone else's address. She kept arguing with me. I hung up and called back and talked to a man who took information down. I was frustrated because we could have gotten them if they had acted more quickly. The lock on the service door was very flimsy, and people could easily come in and out. In one scene I ran back to the house when somebody warned me the women were there again. I told Tom they had been there because everything was yellow—the fabric on the chairs and sofa.

I dreamed about this theft in April. On July 2 of the same year our garage was broken into by thieves who took golf clubs and a hidden credit card. They proceeded to go rapidly from stores to gas stations charging up a storm. Police told us they believed the burglars broke into the service door and opened the main garage door. My neighbor confirmed she noticed the garage door open about 2 a.m. when she took out her dog.

Remember the two dream women or men coming time and again up to the house? The police figured the real crooks drove by the house on several occasions and observed us loading golf clubs into the trunk of the car. Had I been paying attention to the dream and altered my behavior accordingly, I may have avoided the nightmarish aftermath.

A concerning dream I had about a friend, George, alluded to his need for help, but I regretfully missed the message until I reread it a few years later. By that time I knew of the circumstances envisioned in the dream. It reminded me to take messages like this to heart and reach out to the individual in the dream. A phone call takes little effort and may mean a great deal to the subject of your dream. If all is well, you can relax, put your concerns aside and enjoy the chance to catch up on each other's lives.

> My dream: *Went to Atlanta with my friend Caroline to see a customer. She went in and I saw all sorts of people I knew in the lobby. While she was in there I went to the lobby to look for George. I had seen him sitting on a couch and when I looked back he was sleeping and a very heavy person was sitting on top of him. Anyway he was gone.*

I called George several months later when he did not attend a conference where I expected to see him. He told me he had been with his son who had been diagnosed with a brain tumor. I am not sure whether my connections in the health industry could have helped his son, but I regret not acting sooner when the dream intimated George carried a load on his mind.

Not every premonition dream paints a bleak picture. I dreamed an uplifting little snippet about two weeks after my father underwent lung cancer surgery. My dreams teemed with anxiety around that time, as both my parents had been ill. This vignette reassured me things would be okay.

> *Dreamed we were all in a place sitting in lawn chairs—Sandy, mom and I. Dad was out walking with Dave [brother.] We looked down the road and saw Dad coming this way with a dog. He had walked about a mile with Dave and looked good. He had lost a bunch of weight and was very spry. We all jumped up and got in line to hug him. Everyone was crying but it was thrilling to see him physically fit.*

The prophecy happily turned out to be true. Dad's surgery succeeded, and he enjoyed nearly ten more years of life, free from lung cancer.

My saddest premonition dream happened on October 2, 1999. A nightmare frightened me early on a Saturday morning. I bolted out of bed at six-twenty-two, shaking like a leaf. Waking up suddenly is not conducive to journalizing dreams, so I did not capture the particulars, only the essence of the dream. A more gradual awakening, eyes closed, and minimal, if any, light creates the ideal environment for remembering the specifics.

Although I missed details, it had to do with the Left Behind book series by Tim LaHaye and Jerry Jenkins. I had been reading one of the twelve editions in the series having to do with the end of life as we know it. I wrote down in my journal how I felt after the dream—anxious, upset, disturbed—and I had no idea why.

I got up, and an hour later I received a phone call from my father telling me my grandmother passed away.

A dream is a prophecy in miniature.

~ Talmud

10

WARNINGS

Warning dreams have been disclosed for thousands of years, the earliest recorded in the Bible. A familiar story to anyone who attends a Christmas Eve church service is the story of Joseph, who received a message in a dream soon after Jesus' birth. From Matthew, Chapter 2, verse 13: "When they had gone, an angel of the Lord appeared to Joseph in a dream. 'Get up,' he said, 'take the child and his mother and escape to Egypt. Stay there until I tell you, for Herod is going to search for the child to kill him.'"

Herod, King of Judea, felt threatened by the birth of Jesus, as people were calling him King of the Jews, a title Herod thought rightly belonged to himself. Jesus, Joseph, and Mary's lives were threatened. They acted on Joseph's dream, heading for Egypt, avoiding danger.

Warnings in my dreams range from yellow cautionary flags to outright horns and sirens, celestially speaking. More banal than dramatic, a dream might take the form of a simple "head's up."

One such dream:

I worked for an organization in foodservice and took a new job that would require me to work with Trent Lott [senator at the time]. I knew I would have to work with Congress, but that did not worry me. There were a bunch of conversations with people who kept trying to give me advice about getting along there. There were some scenes where people were coming up to me and not aware I had this new position. I was very aware of who was sucking up and who was not. I kept thinking these people would be very transparent, that I could figure out who I really needed and who I did not.

This dream happened shortly after I accepted a new position with a company and would be building an organization from ground up. Very few knew of my plans. I would be in a position to hire a number of people, and interested parties from the competitor lined up to bail out of a merger situation in which their jobs were changing or in jeopardy.

Dream symbolism can be especially clever. In fact, at times it will make you smile when you realize the not-so-subtle hints contained within. Senator Lott—not anyone I would have the occasion to know—and Congress's presence, undoubtedly indicate there would be politics involved. I appreciated the heads up from the messenger, as it confirmed what I already suspected. My task to hire a sales organization would not lack for candidates.

My company's acquisition of its primary competitor provided a backdrop against which vivid dreams took place for well over a year. Hiring and firing, jockeying for positions, and even choosing office locations made for water-cooler conversation by day. At night, my subconscious processed the events and helped me hold tight to my seat on the emotional roller coaster we rode.

I recorded dreams like this one on a regular basis:

We were having a large meeting having to do with the merger, and I would go to one room and get set up, put my papers on the table, and then they would move the meeting to another room. This kept happening. Finally I mentioned to somebody how annoying that was. I went into the room and saw Jerry who told me the meetings were always scheduled for a particular room. I said that did not matter because each time I went there, it had been moved. I had to continually pick up my things and go somewhere else.

No solution appeared in this episode, but I accepted it as a cautionary flag. Buckle up, I told myself, as this roller coaster is going to see a few more hills and drops before it is all done—and it did. Every day brought directional change from leadership in the company, but I felt ready for it.

There are reams of written accounts of those whose dreams alerted them to impending doom. Maybe you have had such a dream. I hope they are few and far between as they are unsettling.

What occurs more often for me, however, are cautionary dreams. They hoist a red flag, signaling something that has not even appeared on my radar screen yet. Often I will awaken from one with a greater sense of urgency for something I put on the back burner. It all depends on whether I get the drift of the message. After years of journaling, my own dream dictionary contains plenty of images to help me decode its contents.

Figures of speech and popular expression are good indications there is a hidden meaning in your dream. Pay heed when you note an obvious cliché in your journal. One example is when I dreamed about a vehicle losing its wheels. Have you heard the expression "the wheels are coming off"? It is an idiom meaning something is all wrong or doomed to fail. Here is an example of the expression in a dream I had during a time when I considered a job offer at a new company:

> *I took a new job and went to the building and found all sorts of things different that I did not like.*

You couldn't get any food in a cafeteria. Someone told me we would be moving from this building to another. I asked where it was and nobody could tell me. They said it would take an act of Congress to get the information. I sat down with Pat, a customer friend of mine, who said she'd show me around. I wanted to know what the president was like. He's a bit argumentative, she said. I could tell this wouldn't be my favorite guy. I went out to my car, and a guy was crouched low as if he was fixing something. I ignored him and got into the car, but my husband stuck his head in the window and said my wheels were missing. I was shocked the guy was able to remove the wheels without my knowing it.

Indeed true, "the wheels were coming off" with the job, and I had not even accepted it yet. The benefit of journalizing proves the accuracy of the warning. I took the position and, just as my dream cautioned, it turned rocky many times during the first several months. The dream accurately foreshadowed an argumentative chief executive. Offices shifted around frequently, and people were constantly moving, lending credence to the reference in the dream about moving buildings. The offices had no cafeteria, and employees drove quite a distance to find a place for lunch.

Did any of these things amount to impending doom? Most certainly not. But in everyday decision making, it provided food for thought. I did not reconsider the job because of the dream; after all, nothing is perfect. It gave me a valuable reality check about the environment in which I would be working. My intuition told me not everything would be hunky dory. I went in with eyes wide open.

How many times have you used the expression "It would take an act of Congress" to get something done? I believe the dream painted a clear picture. Congress is synonymous with politics. Putting the dream images into context, I faced going into a job in a jittery post-acquisition environment, I knew it would be a political minefield.

My first task would be to create an organization, reviewing the employees who were already there and figuring out who else would be needed. Politics would come into play as people vied for the positions. The dream reinforced my gut feeling that it would call for serious planning, and I went into it with full knowledge of the challenge before me.

Warning dreams are a useful tool for keeping watch over your health, as I shared in Chapter 7 Body Sense. They also provide clues to help foster healthy relationships with family, spouses, and friends.

This is especially true when you are dealing with a step family. How many people have been blindsided by extreme behavior of a stepchild, ex-husband, or ex-wife? I have friends who experienced a toxic reaction from one or the other and never did find out what ignited the act.

I experienced my share of contentious episodes with an ex or a stepchild. If you are part of the forty percent of Americans who live in a stepfamily, you know how it is. Money, power, and psychological maneuvers all add up to create a wariness that prevents families from establishing any kind of positive relationship. My husband and I experienced all of the above. I always tried to be respectful when dealing with his ex-wife for his sake, but I never developed a sense of trust because of the predictable shenanigans she pulled over the years.

My husband and I tried to develop a cordial relationship with the ex for the benefit of his three children. We made a couple of visits to their home to attend the kids' events. At one gathering I remember telling my husband that she and I might have been friends if I'd known her friendly side in high school. I started to let down my guard for a year or more, when I had this dream:

> *Dreamed my husband's ex was throwing a party, and I went to her house to try to help. She was stressed out because she couldn't find a caterer. I said I was in the foodservice business, and caterers were my customers; I would bring her names tomorrow. I also thought it would be a good chance to talk to the kids and find out what's happening with them. I*

went out to my car, and as I bent over to put the key in the lock, my mind pictured somebody coming up behind me and grabbing me. A quick thought crossed my mind that I should look around to be sure nobody was behind me. But it was too late. A guy grabbed me around the waist and carried me into the middle of the street. He pushed me down and held me on the road while a big truck came right at me! I struggled, and the driver saw me, slowed down, and I wriggled away in time.

There were times in the past when I dreamed about an unnamed figure I surmised might be her, but until now no dream outright named her in the starring role. Yet the incident seemed plausible, at least metaphorically, and my intuitive radar ramped up. I thought about what might have triggered the dream.

A month later the memory of this dream came roaring back.

A few weeks after the truck-bearing-down-on-me nightmare, my husband rested in a cardiac care unit waiting to have a stent embedded in his artery. The doctor called me in and told us it would not be happening as planned. Since they discovered a significant blockage, he would be scheduled for bypass surgery in a few days. The doctor directed us to go home and get ready.

Heart surgery is almost routine today, but in the year 2000 it frightened us both. A flurry of activity took place, including notification to friends and relatives. My husband called his kids to explain the gravity of the situation. Their reaction? Nonchalant, at best. I thought it a bit odd, as I recalled my own family's experience with my mother's cardiac episodes, and I remembered all too well the anxious moments we endured.

On the day of the surgery I called each of his kids to report on his successful surgery and update them on their father's condition. The response I received? "Oh, okay." As he recovered in the hospital, not one of them called to check in. Finally, he heard from them, but the call did not come to inquire about his progress. Rather, they phoned to tell him about an issue with which their mother was dealing. My anger and hurt for him boiled over. In fact, I felt as if I had been hit by a truck or punched in the gut (recalling the dream scenario) with the ugliness they showed.

We learned a few months later that his ex filled the kids with hateful and false impressions about their father. He deserved none of it. My dream served as a loud warning to keep my vigilance and not be fooled by her phony display of friendliness a year earlier.

Dreams have an astounding way of revealing with keen accuracy the character of a person, much more on target than many people have in their waking hours. If my intuition makes me uneasy about someone, chances are the reason will be revealed in the middle of the night.

Two examples remind me of the validity of warning dreams. I tend to be a person who trusts everyone until they give me a reason to retract my confidence. I appreciate a wake-up call from a well meaning friend or colleague, alerting me to a potential betrayal. Sometimes dreams act as a harbinger.

A short, but revealing, dream warned my partner, Caroline, and me about a business situation about to go awry. In negotiating an agreement with a group of business executives, I approached it as I normally do. I trust the parties' intention to do what is fair and equitable for all. This dream came the night before we were to receive the proposal. Disappointingly, it forewarned me of the outrageously unacceptable offer.

> My dream: *Caroline and I were staying at a hotel and received our statement as we were checking out. We looked at the bill and saw we had been charged $956 for a cup of tea. We looked at each other and said "we're getting screwed."*

Later that very day we received an email from the other parties proposing a stunningly one-sided agreement. In fact, it would have been laughable if it weren't so insulting. Forewarned is forearmed, as the saying goes. We were ready for it and eventually worked out a favorable contract.

As a start-up business owner, I make judgment calls on professional relationships, including with whom to establish partnerships—suppliers, sales representatives, accountants, lawyers and customers. When I entered a new industry, pet supplies, and located to a new city, my established networks were not necessarily the right ones for the new company. I started from scratch.

I met with potential sales reps and brokers, working with some on a commission-only basis to limit the financial exposure until I could be sure I hired the right team. I decided to work with one rep because of her love of dogs, and she needed the work. I like helping young women hone their sales skills, and it seemed like a good match in the beginning. To my chagrin, teaching her the basics took much more time than I expected, yet I continued to try and help her develop. This dream woke me up with a supernatural elbow jab, alerting me to rethink my strategy:

Dreamed I was at Gail's house and was going to take care of a dog. There was a huge snake sitting up cobra style. I hit it, to make it go away, but then there was a smaller kind of worm and it stuck itself to my leg. It was a leech. There were several small babies with it, and they left marks. The dream continued with people trying to find these things and get rid of them but I said there was no way I would stay there.

I admit the leeches could have represented someone other than Gail, and I considered a few possibilities. There were any number of things sucking the life out of me at the time, as the demands of a new business tend to do, but the dog appeared to be the distinguishing feature in this dream, representing the pet supply business. I knew I would have to make a change. Fortunately, Gail met someone new who changed her life, moved her to a new city, and everyone lived happily ever after.

11

THERAPEUTIC DREAMS

Right up front let me say I would never advocate avoiding psychotherapy when you are dealing with a traumatic personal situation. However, in a world where we all too often turn to substances to deal with everyday letdowns, a more positive method of dealing with life's twists and turns is always welcome. I believe dreams have the ability to take it on, as long as you are paying attention and willing to spend some time thinking through their meaning.

Let's take a situation where you need to make a moral decision about something. You know inherently the right answer for you. Effective therapists ask questions and dig deep enough into your psyche that you actually come up with the answer yourself. Dreams behave in a similar fashion.

Sigmund Freud (*The Interpretation of Dreams, circa 1900*) and Carl Jung both studied how dreams reflect subconscious or unconscious thoughts, making them ideal as a tool for psychotherapy. Jung believed we dream about things we have neglected in our waking hours, and the dream acts as an alert to get you to pay attention to the issue of focus in the dream. Other psychologists followed Freud and Jung, with theories that dreams played a vital role in mental health and maintaining stability in relationships.

Where this plays out as a practical matter is the way your dreams make you feel emotionally when you wake up. Did you make a decision in your nightly narrative that made you feel strong and capable the next morning? Through the images in your mind, did you feel a strong pull toward one path versus another?

In Chapter 8, I wrote about my friendship with Matt and the hole it left in my heart when he avoided me following my promotion to a job he vacated when he left the company. The dreams of fiery images signified a transition for me. I moved on but never got over the loss of a treasured friendship.

A month after the fire images appeared, I dreamed what I believe to be a sign of emotional healing from the open wound.

Dreamed I had surgery to remove a growth in a hospital that did not have much in the way of service. They wheeled my bed around and left me in the hallway. In a wheelchair, I had to push with my feet to get it going. They were going to move me to a room, but the hallways were busy, and they couldn't find one. When they did, someone else was already in the room. So they left me in the hallway again. I found my way back and walked with a blanket around me. Nobody paid much attention.

To some, this dream sounds ominous. Surgery is bad enough, without the added annoyance of health professionals ignoring you. There is another way to look at it, and I see it as therapeutic. The symbolism of surgery could signify cutting away something bad. This dream not only allows me to remove a "malignancy," but it also depicts a strong, self sufficient person pushing her chair along without assistance. As in other dreams, I threw in a security blanket for reassurance. Overall, the dream left me with a positive feeling.

This is why I suggest you must be willing to take some time with a dream. Mull it over, and consider different explanations for the symbolism it holds. Remember, you are the one who passes final judgment on the meaning.

During a challenging time in my life I had a series of three dreams, one right after another. As I wrote down the third dream, I realized the three composed a complete picture. The message, taken in its entirety, provides a perspective like that of a therapist lending counsel. As you read each of these dreams, see if your interpretation changes as you move from one to the next.

My first dream: *Dreamed I left a company and needed to get my things out of my office. I had so much stuff in there. A friend suggested we get it all out tonight rather than waiting for the last couple days of work. We hauled out three sets of golf clubs, two Christmas trees, and photos pinned to a bulletin board. I left an antique teacup which somebody said their daughter bought from my consignment store; I thought she should have it. I packed a piece of a banister which I thought would make a good weapon. I loaded everything into a fire truck. I drove it through the halls, and someone was helping me steer it through the doorways to get it out. I drove over a railing and was laughing about it with friends saying they would probably get blamed for doing it. I drove as if I did not give a damn. At the end of the hall there were stairs. I looked up and saw my friend, Rick. He invited me up for drinks and Chinese appetizers, and we laughed.*

Dream two: *Dreamed I was getting ready to leave my company again, and I was there for final meetings. The assistant had me type a label for a file using white tape. I said I could handle it on my Selectric typewriter. It took me a couple tries because the ink was not very good on the typewriter, and the letters were too big for the little white tape. In walked three guys who told me we needed to go to another building. As we walked through the garage one guy said it was very nostalgic because that's where my predecessor used to park. All three men jumped up on unicycles, and there was one for me, too. I declined; said I would walk, but then I decided to give it a try. The darn thing did not have a seat on it, just a pipe that you hung onto and balanced over the wheel. I got on and started riding. I asked them how things were going, and they all said it was just the same.*

Dream three: *I was supposed to make a presentation on my company's business plan. There was a pile of jewelry on the table in front of me. That night there would be a banquet. Next to me on the left was Dan and the right was my high school boyfriend. People came up and said good things, that I was helping them with their businesses, etc. Suddenly Dan gave me a hug and said he was happy for me that everything was going well. I was shocked and kept cleaning up and getting ready for the next presentation. Then my old boyfriend gave me a big hug. I said what was that for? He said," no, really come here," and gave me a giant hug. I looked surprised. He said he was proud of me for helping people and wanted me to know. He almost made me cry.*

I hope you are now at the point where you are attempting your own quick analysis of what the series of dreams tries to bring forth. To help you unearth its meaning for me, let's take it one image at a time to understand the symbolism.

In Dream One I mention *the consignment store.* What is a consignment store's general purpose? It is to find a home for something when the first owner no longer needs it. I think it meant I no longer needed the job. No emotional goodbyes necessary—time to move on.

I loaded everything into a fire truck. Remember from Chapter 8 that fire for me represents transition. What would a fire truck represent? It could be good or bad for someone who is leaving a job depending on the circumstances of departure.

In this case my journal said *I drove as if I did not give a damn.* Sounds like someone with no regrets about leaving, does it not? Add to that the chuckle I shared with my friend, Rick. I have known him for thirty years, and we have shared many conversations about jobs and bosses over the years. Just as good friends are there for you in good times and bad, Rick's appearance in the dream for me is comforting.

Dream Two has some interesting symbolism represented by old-fashioned white tape and a Selectric® typewriter with bad ink. How many years ago did those become obsolete? As a former typing teacher, I know what this means. I recorded the dream in 2009, long after the Selectric took up residence at the Smithsonian. The company I left is wallowing in the past, not a forward thinking company. My dream guides reminded me it is not a place I wanted to be. The unicycle perhaps represents a balancing act. Much later, after I moved on to start my own business, the meaning crystallized.

Dream Three contains a pile of jewelry. Being a lover of all things "bling," and knowing experts interpret jewelry to represent pearls of wisdom, I sense the Universe telling me there will be riches—physical or emotional—on the other side.

The boss on the far left and my old boyfriend on the far right signify polar opposites. Can you tell what is on the spectrum? The hugging scene shows feigned appreciation on one end, true pride and acknowledgment on the other. In real life, my opinion of the individual's character is precisely what appeared in the dream. An insincere compliment from Dan advised me not to spend too much time worrying about him anymore.

The timing of this series of dreams is why I classify them as "therapy" for me. I left the corporate world for entrepreneurship, and as many small business owners know, the first year is formidable. Ebbs and flows in sales and time being sucked up by nonrevenue producing activities will make many people occasionally question whether they made the right decision to go out on their own.

During the greatest mental boxing matches with myself, I find dreams like this popping up to buoy my confidence or guide me in a new direction. The three dreams fall into the reassurance category because of the insights I gained.

Sometimes dreams portray me doing something cathartic, such as driving away in a car, leaving the past or an ugly situation behind. There are also instances where I feel directed to do nothing. Either way, I get a distinct sense to do one or the other. The dream does not usually leave the situation in an ambiguous state.

One nighttime narrative assisted me with a decision I had to make about a former coworker, Richard. I previously admired him as an industry colleague, until he and I ended up employed by the same company. During the time we worked together, I discovered our values were diametrically opposed, and I tacitly questioned his ethics on numerous occasions.

When I left the company, for some reason I felt as though I needed closure with him. I saw him at industry functions several times and tried to approach him. Each time something or someone interrupted, and I never got the chance to say anything. It bothered me, as I like to tie things up with a pretty bow and leave relationships in a positive state. I did not know if that would mean anything to him. It might have been all my issue.

This dream provided the direction I needed with regard to my relationship with Richard:

> *My friend, Caroline, and I went to an office building to see Richard. We saw all sorts of people we knew in the lobby and ended up in conversation with many. I finally decided to ask if I could see Richard and clear the air. His assistant wanted to know why I wanted to see him, and I said I just wanted to know if he would give his blessing for me to work with him or his people again. She disappeared. She took so long that Caroline came out of her appointment, and we decided to leave. We got in her car and we*

decided they were just making me wait to show Richard's power in making people bow down to him. In the car Caroline showed me a book she was writing, and it had clippings from magazines and newspapers pasted to pages. I told her she should publish it, and she said "see, I was writing about him long ago."

Caroline is a trusted friend, and someone whose opinion I value. This appearance in the dream cemented her real-life advice. She told me I should not worry about him ever again. His power trips were not worthy of my attention, and the dream reinforced her advice. It freed me from a nagging thought-bubble each time I ran into him from then on. Thank you, Dr. Caroline.

Sometimes a "therapy dream" happens to me when I need to wake up, mentally or spiritually. Do you ever feel the business of life preventing you from taking care of the most important things? You find yourself running from one task to another. Perhaps you don't listen to your spouse or children as carefully as you should. You may not even realize it until your family and friends bristle each time you enter the room. When I find myself in a similar phase, I lean on my dreams to help me recognize when I am distracted from priorities.

"Workaholism" has been one such syndrome for me in the past and for many friends of mine. It feeds something inside of me. I get an adrenalin rush from it, and pretty soon my entire life is consumed by work, to the detriment of relationships I treasure. Every now and then I require a rap on the noggin from someone I care about to let me know I have crossed the threshold into a single dimension.

One such wake-up call came during a particularly intense phase of my corporate career. The dream went like this:

Dreamed I had forgotten my name. I was asking people what it was and trying to retrace my steps to places I had been to get a clue. At the same time, someone had stolen jewelry and other things of mine, so I was looking for those as well. One of my neighbors showed me some drawers in her house and said a guy had taken my things and put them there. She showed me some tongs, small dishes and a bracelet. I called some friends to come over and help me look for more things. Then I couldn't remember when they were coming. I never did recover my name.

Forgetting my name troubled me. Symbolically, my very identity could be in question. The jewelry and other possessions depicted things of value in my life that were stolen—or perhaps given away. Remember, too, that jewelry represents wisdom. Had mine been stolen? Household gadgets may represent a facet of home life such as dining together as a family. This dream told me it was time to start paying attention to something other than work.

The question of identity comes up from time to time in my dreams. It seems my subconscious is trying to help me find my purpose and keep all things in balance. I don't have children, but I imagine those who do can identify with the struggle of wearing many hats. Which one are you wearing today? Mom or Dad? Husband or wife? Lover? Teacher? Employee or employer? Business owner? Coach?

Each of us plays a myriad of roles. Hopefully we see clearly which one should take the lead each day and particularly at important junctures in life. If the picture is murky for you, read through your dream journal for guidance. I received a heavy dose of reality with this dream:

> *I was at an outdoor gathering of people I knew from various jobs and they were giving out awards and prizes. I went over to talk to Susie [a sorority sister] and asked her how many times her cell phone made a "butt call" to me. We laughed about it, and I said I was happy to hear from her. We were interrupted when a man came to get me and said "they want you over here." I went back to where the festivities were going on, but nobody was there. In another area a woman was being honored because she was "graduating." I told her I remembered when she*

started school, and it made me feel old. A few other people were there and so was Tom [a former employee]. I was reminiscing about how well each had turned out. Then I went back to the stage area and saw a box of giant Elton John glasses with my name on them. Inside the glasses was a piece of paper that folded out. A woman came by and told me it contained a caricature. I pulled out the paper. Sure enough, only mine had not just one—it had 4 panels of different caricatures with 4 titles on it—teacher and activist were the only two that stood out. I was trying to figure out what the other two were, as they were blurry.

The dream left a considerable impression on me. The caricatures were disconcerting. I usually bristle at being labeled as one thing or another. I prefer to be seen as a multi-dimensional person with flexibility to adapt to my circumstances. The idea of caricatures made me think some element of my personality was being exaggerated over something else.

Teacher and activist are not bad roles to play, but where were the roles I played in my personal life? Per the dream, that part of the paper was illegible. The dream, I believed, meant they did not stand out, overshadowed by the roles of teacher and activist.

The Elton John glasses—a caricature in themselves—provided the means to seeing things more clearly. They were labeled with my name, suggesting, perhaps, that I needed to take a look at reprioritizing my life. As I think about it, the song *I Can See Clearly Now* runs through my mind. I find it constructive when a therapeutic dream shows up, just to help me maintain mental or emotional balance.

Therapeutic dreams don't always speak of trouble. I dream joyfully when life is going well, and I hope you do, too. It is exhilarating to wake up with a fresh image of being on top of the world.

I recall a short, but pleasant dream during a time everything seemed to be going in the right direction for me in and outside of work. My job and company were secure, and sales successes were accumulating. I served on two prestigious boards at my alma mater, and I had been named Distinguished Alumna at the University. My home life rolled along; I enjoyed family and friends. Life's demands appeared to be in harmony.

> My dream: *I dreamed I piloted a plane by myself, with an open cockpit over water and a city. I wasn't afraid at all, just pleased I was able to do it. When I landed it, I came to the conclusion I didn't like it, and I realized I did not need to do that to prove anything. So I told the people who owned the plane that I wouldn't be doing that any longer.*

I finally made it, I thought. Rather than continuing to soar for greater achievements, I acquired the elusive balance I sought.

Therapeutic dreams can offer support for tumultuous times such as when dealing with illness or the death of loved ones. There are also times when the dead appear in a dream, and it has nothing to do with that person at all.

It may be a reflection of something that died within you.

Dream expert Tony Crisp explains, "This [dreams of death] can represent some area of your life that has 'died'. It can refer to death of feelings, such as hopelessness in connection with relationship and the loss of feelings about someone; the depression that follows big changes in your life such as loss of a loved partner, job, or child. It can also reflect the sense you have of your life in general, that it is without the stimulus of motivation and satisfaction, as when one feels oneself in a 'going nowhere' relationship or life situation. The dead person in the dream may link several of these feelings together, as symbols often represent huge areas of our experience. So the dead person may be a part of oneself you want to leave behind, to die out."

My dreams typically contained images like this when major transitions took place at work. One year our company laid off dozens of people. My intuition warned me of their "death" when I had this dream a few weeks before "Black Friday."

I was in a wide winged airplane and it was going to crash, but as it came in close to the ground it very gracefully lowered itself and I was able to step out of the top of it. I ran from the crash. Many other people died. There was a baby and I ran up and hugged the baby because I was so happy we were alive.

In this case, the deaths were job losses. I interpreted the baby's role to be that of a fairly new employee of mine who escaped the layoffs.

Some death-related dreams are therapeutic. I will share two of them with you, both of which occurred in the same month. One starred my Aunt Evelyn, who passed away from Alzheimer's six months before the dream occurred. The other one held significance for me, as it was the first time I dreamed about my mother since her passing three years earlier.

Dreamed about Auntie Ev, that she was being cared for in a beautiful facility, and some friends and I were there. I was concerned she wouldn't recognize me. There was a large knife taped to her bed. So far so good that she recognized me. She said something about Tom [husband] traveling and I said yes, he probably was, and she said he would be in a big metal plane somewhere. She came up to me and hugged me. I started crying. She handed me the knife, which to everybody in the room meant that she was okay, that she wouldn't hurt herself, and she had her mind back because she remembered Tom would be traveling and knew what a plane was. My friend said, "see, everything is okay now." I just kept rocking her and crying because I knew she was alright again.

Toward the end of her life, my aunt's disease caused her to revert to acting like a small child, forgetting things a typical adult should know. She and I were close, and I admired her since my teen years for her competence in the business world and the glamorous trips she and my uncle used to take. Alzheimer's not only robs the person suffering from the dreaded disease, it also steals from family members who watch the person they know and love slip away.

My aunt's final months distressed me when I recalled episodes I witnessed in the nursing home. My dream granted me a sense of relief, as its heavenly message for me confirmed her disease no longer tormented her. Her mind revealed clear thinking. She seemed to be in good hands.

The dream about my mother is an example of one I believe falls under the genre described by Tony Crisp. My "guides" used her image to reveal something about me.

The dream:

Mom and I were at a beautiful resort, and we were walking back to where everyone else in the family had gathered. She and I were just strolling when I realized I forgot my purse and I said "oh no, I left it in the car." Mom was dragging a big purse, as she always did when she was alive, and said she did not know what she would do without her purse because everything she needed was in it. She told me I did not need to get my purse because she had what I would need.

The common element between the two dreams is that they both took place in lovely surroundings—*a beautiful resort/facility.* As a Christian, this image reinforced my belief in life after death. I picked up another spiritual message from mother to daughter: She has eternal peace. I do not have to worry about all the earthly baggage (the purse), as Mom already has a handle on what I will need when I see her again.

12

DREAMS I WISH I HAD ACTED UPON

I do not want to leave you with the impression that every time I dream it points me to a path, or that I pay attention and implement every directional message successfully in my life. There are occasions when I dream something disturbing and chalk it up to something I ate or a bad movie and ignore it for the time being.

The benefit of journaling for decades comes one day when something happens and you remember you once dreamed about it. It is a bit like déjà vu, only you did not experience it, you simply dreamed about it and wrote it down. When you have volumes of dreams in your library you can go back to verify that it is not your imagination. Celestial hindsight is twenty-twenty.

You may recall from Chapter 1 my story about Dick and how I dreamed about his stay in the intensive care unit on his wedding day. I wish I gave that particular dream more credence. I might have been a source of support for Dick during those dark days.

There have also been times, thankfully not many, in which I dreamed about an event or a person and completely missed the message, because its implausibility did not warrant a second thought. Cities and airports post public awareness signs, "If you see something, say something." Here are a few times when I wish I had.

My dream: *Dreamed that Lynn [a childhood friend] was holding everybody hostage, that we were all in a room and she was going to start shooting if we left. My brother-in-law, Tom, got away and he was out looking for the authorities. My sister, Sandy, and I were sitting in the room and every time we got ready to move Lynn threatened us. Finally I saw she looked vulnerable and I held my arms open to her for a hug and she came over and hugged and cried. The episode was over and she gave up.*

I thought about the dream and tried to connect Lynn and her personality traits with someone in my current life. I had not seen her in many years, as she lived in my home state halfway across the country. Any traits of Lynn's I might try to apply to someone in my life today would be a guess based on thirty-five year old memories.

I could not reconcile it, so the dream ended up in the big red dream box without a note of explanation, as clues were scarce. It bothered me to see Lynn in a vulnerable position, but there did not seem to be a message I could get my mind around.

About two years after the dream occurred, I received a call telling me Lynn passed away. Unbeknownst to me she suffered for quite some time with cancer. It troubles me to this day that I had not been in touch with her for many years, and I was unaware of what she had been going through. In fact, I still do not know whether the cancer had been diagnosed at the time I had the dream, which makes it even more disturbing. Could it have been a vision of what she endured? I am usually the person who picks up the phone and calls someone when they cross my mind, in waking hours or celestially. This is one time I wish I had done so.

A similar situation happened a little more than two years before Bruce, a good friend and co-worker, passed away from leukemia. Here is what I dreamed about him:

I was in a lab at work, talking to somebody who was going to show me some confidential information. I looked around the lab and saw somebody coming around the corner wearing a company logo hat. I thought it was a colleague named Lou, so I asked this person to wait, and I went to give Lou a hug, but it turned out to be Bruce instead. He looked so different and was so puffy. I told him he looked good the last time I saw him. As he started talking, his face kept changing. In fact, at one point he looked like a woman and talked about how he was sending his mail to other people for handling.

I wrote in my journal that I visited him a week before, and he did not look well. I commented "Bruce is morphing into a different life form before my sleeping eyes. Dear God, I pray this isn't some kind of omen, and that he can beat the illness."

A year later, about fourteen months before Bruce passed away, I dreamed about him:

Dreamed Bruce was in a little office nearby and was writing out invitations to his funeral. I was upset, and he said it was ok, that he had come to grips with things and he needed to get it done.

Over the next several months I thought no news was good news and dismissed the dreams as my emotional reaction to his illness. I talked with him several times, but he did not want to see anyone. I thought he beat it until I received the call telling me of his passing. I missed him immediately. He had a great sense of humor and a devil-may-care attitude during his working years, which I admired.

My regret is that I had two years following my providential morphing dream, and there were things I wanted to say. We chatted about light topics on the phone, but I did not take the opportunity to tell him I wish I could be more like him and let job pressures slide, like water off a duck's back.

13

ADVISORY BOARD

Dream experts devote lots of time to analyzing recurring dreams or repeated symbols within the story. I shared my own dream themes in Chapter 6. Equally important in my dreams is the recurrence of certain characters. I have come to know them as my advisors because of the roles they play and places they show up.

My church leaders are a good example. I am fortunate to have been blessed with terrific pastors throughout the years. Pastors Peter, Karen, and David made regular appearances in my dreams during the years I attended Lord of Life Church in Maple Grove, Minnesota.

A frequent and meaningful image of me laying my head on the lap of a pastor brought me comfort when I felt a weighty problem on my mind. A typical scene depicts me lost in a parking lot or airport or involved in a chase. Out of the blue my pastor enters the picture, and I lay my head on his lap. He does not even say anything, but I wake up feeling as though everything will be okay.

Pastor Peter's image arose in a dream the day after my father received a diagnosis of lung cancer. I believe the message related to our family's moving through the initial shock to plan for what would come next.

> The dream:*We were in a church and Pastor Peter was there. Mom was there but not dad. There were 3 containers that were labeled, and the middle one was labeled Kids Advance. Peter was pulling name tags out of it and putting them on people. He pulled one out to put on mom. As I woke up I remembered thinking this was a dream telling us things would be ok.*

If you have a spiritual guide in your life, I expect she or he passes through your dreams in a helpful way. In this dream, it appeared to me that the pastor blessed the journey for us— *Kids Advance.* Perhaps the identity of your advisor is not as obvious as mine. If you cannot identify anyone, I encourage you to look for people who appear multiple times. It may take several months, or even years, of journaling for their roles to emerge.

Other frequent guests on the dream circuit are my parents. Typically they do not play a "starring" role, but there they are in my journal in countless dreams. I describe an activity and the description inevitably includes "mom and dad were there." It is as if they represent my conscience or parental instincts—always a factor in making judgment calls. Sometimes there is a lead role for one of them, such as the time I dreamed we were living in the 1950s, and my dad wore white shoes and plaid pants as a successful salesman. Who said dreams do not include an occasional stereotype to make a point?

Experts say dreaming about your parents has little to do with them *per se*. It has more to do with parental traits within yourself. Either way, when my mother and father appear I instinctively know what it means. There could be an element of protectionism, but more often than not, they serve as a reminder to make good decisions. "Use your own judgment," is what I hear in the back of my mind, with the unheard rejoinder, "and it better be the right one."

A frequent guest star in dreams I have recorded since the beginning of my journaling expedition is Gary, a high school classmate and sweetheart. According to Lauri Quinn Loewenberg in *Dream On It*, classmates are on the top-ten list of people we dream about, but it is not because they are on our minds frequently. Rather, it is because you remember something about them you may or may not see in yourself.

If the person exhibits extreme generosity, for example, you may secretly wish you could be more giving. On the other hand, Loewenberg says, it works both ways. You may also recognize your shared trait as a problem in certain circumstances, such as when generosity becomes a way for people to take advantage of you.

What do you remember about a former classmate who keeps showing up in your dreams? I gave it some serious thought in an attempt to figure out why Gary drops in so often.

He is a guy who marches to the beat of his own drum. In school he did not conform to what everybody else did. He listened to his own music, watched movies nobody else cared about, and revered icons on which no other male wasted his time. "Comfortable in his own skin," is how people would have described him forty-some years ago. I admire how he did not let others' opinions overtly influence how he lived life.

Here is a journal excerpt in which he appeared.

> *Dreamed I was doing a business project with Caroline and we needed some endorsements. I asked Gary to come and hear me out. He came to my house, I told him about the project and was shy about asking him but he said he would endorse it. There was a very loving scene where he hugged and kissed me. I told Caroline I had wanted all along to get his approval but thought I never would, and here it happened. There was also a funny scene where he was sitting next to me and I remarked about his big feet. They were huge shoes. Then I started telling Caroline about how*

much I wanted to get his endorsement. I started to say he knew what I was going through and Ray stepped in and said abruptly, "nobody knows what you are going through" and I was taken aback because I thought he was negative about the project.

Symbolically, the loving scene tells me we were to get a seal of approval on our project. Despite any trepidation we felt about the direction we were going, Gary's affirmation meant something to me. In fact, living up to his standards of being your own person also displayed itself in the clever metaphor about footwear. He has big shoes to fill, indicating the endorsement did not come lightly. Caroline and I moved forward with the project, and we were both pleased with the result.

Gary, the advisor, does not always nod his head in agreement with my decision making. About fifteen years ago a company approached me with a job offer I considered to be a lateral one, but they positioned it as one with enormous upside potential. By now you probably guessed I had several dreams about it during the weeks of interviews and back-and-forth conversations. Not surprisingly, one of them starred Gary.

Dreamed I was renewing a relationship with Gary. He called and I was all excited. I was living with Dave [brother] and he was making fun of me saying I was acting silly because I was gaga over him. I was in an office building and a young girl would be working for me who was very energetic. She turned on a radio in the office, and I said we have never had a radio on in my office and it was so good to hear music. I was going to give her some objectives to see what she could do because I thought she had energy, but she might not do any work. After a few office scenes where she was showing off her energy I was on a bike with a woman and a black man and we were riding in a city in an area that was not so good. He mentioned it might be Indy. I asked him how long it would take me to ride "home" to

San Antonio. He said it would not take long if I could get on a plane. Then I started to panic because I realized I must have ridden much farther than I thought. I was anxious to get back to Gary. I called Dave and asked him if I had any calls. He told me about one woman who called about a job and said, "the bus was full this time so I would have to come back again later," but no call from Gary.

I think this dream is so full of warning flags, it would be difficult to miss the cautionary message. I should not take the job. The woman in the dream displayed both good qualities and questionable motives. She added an element to the office scene—music. I am such a music lover this could represent an attractive element in the new company.

The other characters in the dream piqued my interest. It just so happened one of the key players at the company courting me is black. The phrase *I must have ridden much farther than I thought* could be a signal I took things too far with the potential new job.

The dream shows I hurried back to try and get Gary's take on things, and he did not call. At first it took me a few minutes to analyze whether the bus being full is a good or bad sign. Even with a promising reference to the new company, it just is not enough to overcome the downside. If the "bus is full," there may be a fight for the seat I really wanted. I did not take the job, and a few months later I received a promotion and moved on to an exciting new adventure in my company. Good call.

At least one of my advisors is always present, and it is especially revealing when more than one enters the same celestial room. A dream, shortly after the birth of my nephew, Michael, featured appearances by my sister, our parents, and the high school classmate, and it focused on my decision not to have children. A few times over the years, especially around milestone birthdays or when my sister or sister-in-law presented a new face to the family, I would go over the dilemma mentally and wonder if I made the right decision to forego having children. The answer always came back, yes.

My dream: *Gary and I were visiting our home town. Mom and dad lived in a condo building and we were in the party room cleaning up and throwing huge bags of garbage away. Must have been one big party. Sandy [sister] and Tom [brother-in-law] were there with Michael [their new baby]. Sandy and a few others started telling stories about the old days and we had drinks and a good time. Gary was very friendly. I had several chances to talk with him privately and I told him I missed him. He said the same. When I asked him how he was doing he said "just hanging out, sleeping, and eating." It appeared as if he was not married anymore. We played with Michael and then everybody was going to go. I started walking him to the door and asked him to keep in touch more often. He said it was difficult but he would try. Then everybody went upstairs and I said I would bring Michael up with me. Gary and I kissed goodbye but then we decided to go for a ride so I put Michael in a backpack and we got into Gary's car. He told me about his apartment and we drove past a large building that is all glass on the front and it was round. He said they had moved out and as of tomorrow he would be somewhere else. I looked up and saw nice apartments through the windows but he said they were not nice. We went back to the condo and Sandy and Tom and mom and dad came down wondering where I was with Michael. They all saw Gary and said how nice it was to see him. They took Michael to go back upstairs and Gary and I discussed getting back together. Gary said he had a good job and it paid three times what his roommates made. I told him there were plenty of chocolate companies in Minneapolis. He said there were a lot of companies in Milwaukee, too, where I could work. It was evident in the dream he was divorced and did not have his kids with him. The whole tone of the dream was very emotional and I felt a longing to be with him. I watched him play with Michael and thought he was probably a very good father. I was doing everything I could to convince him to stay around, or at least to keep in touch more often.*

I restrained myself with this dream, as it is tempting to jump to a conclusion because of the purported happy ending. The good time in the party room, people reminiscing about good times, and the bonding between Gary, the baby, and me coalesce to paint a lovely family picture.

In reality, Gary's life seems perfect. His children, smart and successful, inherited his good looks. Layer this over the dream, and I might conclude I am missing the good life by not having children or a life that mirrored his.

Since Gary's role in my dreams is advisory, I wondered if another message could be gleaned from this excerpt. There are some hints in the middle which expose another side—the not-so-nice looking apartment, the boredom of hanging out, sleeping and eating. Do not miss the reference to a high paying job and plenty of chocolate!

I believe in the end the dream reaffirmed my decision to focus on career. The inevitable euphoria of welcoming a new family member momentarily wormed its way into my nightly visions. Things worked out, as I am a proud aunt to a niece and four nephews who bring joy to my life and keep me laughing.

Out of all the advisors who contribute to my day-to-day problem solving, there is one who holds the title of chairman of the advisory board—my sister, Sandy. Explicit patterns emerge in my journal supporting the premise. Each advisor has a specific role. My sister's is to be there no matter what, and she reliably shows up, not infrequently.

During my corporate career, as I studied women in leadership roles, I read much about creating your own "board of advisors." Gurus speak about surrounding yourself with coaches who will tell you the truth about how you are perceived in the business community.

Mentoring programs have sprung up to assist women in pursuing coveted "c-suite" positions. I, too, trust a small circle of friends to give me feedback and point out where I might be veering off the proper path. My own family plays a significant role on my board.

My celestial coaches do not have to know the nitty gritty of my daily grind to be effective. You have read some accounts of how pastors, parents and classmates do a fine job advising me without even knowing they are doing so. My college friend, Nancy, shows her presence in quiet ways. Even though she and I see each other only once or twice a year, her name is all over my journal. *I had to walk through a parking lot to find Sandy and Nancy. Sandy and Nancy and I were at a party and the Vikings were there. Sandy and Nancy and I were at an airport trying to find the gate.* The two of them act as cheerleaders and a moral compass, letting me know when I am on the right track or treading on thin ice.

Sandy, as my most permanent advisor, makes at least a cameo appearance in most of my dreams. She is there so frequently I initially glossed over her presence until I reread more than nine hundred dreams recorded over a thirty-year period and recognized an emerging pattern. Remarks such as "and Sandy was there," or "Sandy and I were at the airport/house/store" repeat themselves throughout my journal.

She and I are as close as sisters can get, and I have come to realize through my look-back that her presence in my dreams is a critical element to helping me make decisions. A dream like the one to follow reminds me she is with me in spirit even if she does not play a major role in the drama.

> *Dreamed I was in a very low vehicle, like a sled, and Sandy and some others were in another one just behind me. We were driving through a neighborhood, and I was telling her about a house that was slimy and had reptiles in the yard and it was very swampy. All of a sudden, we were in front of it. The yard looked like a swamp and had mulch all over it. I said "here it is—there are probably snakes in that yard." Just then I saw one slither out and come towards my sled. I jumped out to try to run,*

but the snake got tangled up in my feet and I kicked it away. It jumped at me, and I grabbed the back of its head, and it bit me in the hand. It left a V mark on my wrist that looked like it came from a chicken's beak or where an IV would have been. My hand actually started hurting in my sleep. I ran into a medical building, but they said it was the wrong kind of medical and they couldn't help me, that I would have to go to a hospital. Sandy and I got into a car and started driving, and I realized I did not know where I was going, I was just looking for a hospital sign. I could feel my heart racing as if poison was in my system. When I woke, I went to the bathroom and realized my heart was racing and my hand hurt as if I had been bitten for real.

This dream took place during a particularly difficult time for me health-wise. Symptoms proliferated, and I put off going to the doctor because of work obligations. It finally got to the point where I had to have it checked out. Preliminary lab tests showed elevated CA125 markers, one method of detecting ovarian and breast cancers. It frightened me. I just lost an employee to ovarian cancer the year before, and her death weighed heavily on my mind. Breast cancer permeated my family genes, so to mitigate the risk doctors recommended a hysterectomy.

My health problems were exacerbated by a stressful situation at work. I received the call from the lab while attending a trade show, and I spent a sleepless night on the computer researching CA125.

Next morning I worked the show, smiling at customers between stabbing bouts of pain. To my chagrin, I could not hide my suffering. My malevolent boss, working the show with me, told me I should tough it out rather than leave the show early to fly home and see a doctor. Less than twenty-four hours later I ended up in the emergency room.

I am convinced the swamp dream signified a warning that, indeed, the "snake-boss" did not have my best interests at heart. I added it to the growing list of reasons why I needed to part company with him. My sister went everywhere I did in the dream—dodging snakes, racing to the hospital, and navigating swamps.

For political reasons and to shield my employees from "the snake's" abuse, I told very few people about my health scare. Sandy, as she often did, played the role of sustainer—in reality and in nightly visions—during a time I felt very much alone. I hope you have someone who appears in your dreams as comforter, booster, pillar of support. If you pay faithful attention, you may find you have an entire board of advisors.

My sister not only provides moral support in my dreams, but she is also head cheerleader. She does not even need to know the particulars of a real-life drama; she just jumps into the middle of the dream and roots for me.

If you ever felt like David taking on Goliath, I encourage you to look for characters in your dreams who are members of your fan club. Journalizing in detail, including names, is important, as you can easily gloss over someone who appears to play a bit part but may turn out to be a guardian angel of sorts.

Here is a classic cheerleader appearance for Sandy. During a time I worked with a particularly demanding customer, I recorded many dreams that guided me through the process of figuring out how to win him over. My sister did not know this company and never met any of its leaders. Yet this dream displayed her support for my decision to have a heart-to-heart discussion with Mick, the vice president.

> *Dreamed I was at a large meeting and Mick was about to speak. I threw a pencil at him to get his attention and said, "We need a pain management program." Mick proceeded to argue, making fun of people in pain, saying in a sarcastic, whiny voice, "Oh sure, maybe we should have a class so I can feel the pain, too." I couldn't stand it, so I got up and walked right over to him and gave him a lecture about why we need a pain management class. I said there were people out there who were in*

great pain and needed help. It was quite an impassioned speech, and he sat there with his mouth open listening to me. I finished the speech and came back to my chair and Sandy said "way to go!"

I knew immediately from her presence in this dream she was advising me not to procrastinate in having the conversation with the contentious customer. As much as I wanted to avoid a potentially painful confrontation, I sucked it up, called Mick, and we worked things out.

Another dream in which Sandy appeared is eerily prophetic. This one occurred ten years before I became an employee for a particular company. I thought about working for the company, as I knew many people there and thought they were well run. In it, she warned me about going there, as did another co-worker. It turned out they were both right.

I dreamed I visited [the company name] and when I got home I was standing by the front door and thought I saw a dark figure outside. I went to push the door closed the whole way and a hand

233

pushed it toward me. When I opened the door there was Pat, the marketing manager from our retail division, outside my door. I asked him what he was doing there. He said he came to tell me that things are not always greener on the other side of the street. I went upstairs and found Sandy in our old bedroom. She was sitting on the floor playing with something and I told her what happened to me and she said the same thing Pat said.

When my sister appears in my dream, I pay attention to what she "says," as it's usually advice worth heeding.

14

CHIEF ADVISOR

Have you ever wondered whether God/Jesus or the Universe ever picks up your call? Even a person of strong faith, which I consider myself to be, likes a little reassurance every now and then, not only that He hears you and knows what your issues are, but he is invariably sending signals back to you that He received the message. My dreams consistently depict images of Jesus showing up in various scenes. How do I know? By paying attention to the specific words recorded in my journal immediately upon waking up.

The Bible is clear and consistent about Jesus' occupation as he wandered throughout Judea and around the Sea of Galilee. He made his living as a carpenter, just a regular guy. My journals are rich with descriptions, and often I will make reference to "a blue-collar type guy." He is usually helping me out of a tough spot or lending a hand. Often, the figure comforts me in some way. I believe He is Jesus.

One such dream occurred during a stressful time at the office. My corporation acquired another, and many of our jobs were in jeopardy. I, like many others, interviewed with other companies. If you have ever been in a similar situation you may have felt a twinge of guilt over "betraying" your employer, yet it felt necessary to protect your interests should the powers-that-be decide to eliminate your job. That is precisely my frame of mind when I had this dream:

I was in church walking around barefoot, and there were mice everywhere. Most of them dead, some half dead, and they were different colors. The ugliest one was teal. I was jumping all around trying to avoid them as people were moving furniture. There was a blue collar type guy, very nice, who was pushing me on a chair all over the place, through the halls and on sidewalks. Each time we would get to a quiet place, he would hug me. This guy pushed me into a neighborhood, past houses where people were inside looking out. I was afraid they would recognize me. Finally he pushed me into a large family room and stopped the chair. He was going to hug me again when I looked over and saw my sister and sister-in-law sleeping on the couch.

The dead or half-dead mice symbolized the employees who were either let go or soon to be laid off, hence, the different colors. It piqued my interest the ugliest was teal. You may recall from Chapter 4 dream images painted in teal in my dreams signify spirituality, loyalty, trustworthiness. A loyal employee might fare worse than anyone (*the ugliest*) because he remained fiercely dependent rather than take steps to protect his future.

I witnessed behavior in at least a half dozen acquisition scenarios at five companies. The tug of war between maintaining fierce loyalty to the firm and looking out for one's career pulled at each of us daily for as long as the acquisition played itself out. During those times countless good and loyal people lost their jobs as those in charge continued to "move the furniture."

The blue-collar guy, who I see as Jesus, carried my burden by pushing me through the mess in a chair and finally left me in the capable hands of Sandy and Juliet, my sister in law. The symbolism in this dream called out to me to stop worrying about the interview.

I thought about this dream repeatedly and discussed it with a dream-believer friend during that stressful time. We agreed it gave us comfort and clean consciences while looking for another job.

When your Chief Advisor shows up in dreams, it is helpful if you recognize him or her. The lesson I learned over many years of journaling, and I have repeated throughout this book, is to pay attention to detail. Your Advisor may not show up as a guardian angel or a religious figure, and Jesus does not always show up in a white robe. I pay close attention to the descriptions I write in the first few moments upon waking. This is when the images are most vivid and memorable. They are almost more revealing than the activity taking place. Note how I describe the man in the elevator in this post:

> *I was walking down a street, trying to find my way back to my hotel room, and it was getting dark. There were creepy guys following me. All of a sudden a guy grabbed my arm. I must have looked panicky. He said very gently, "Do not worry. I will help you get back safely." He guided me back to the resort, and I immediately grew very fond of him. He was blond with soft facial features. We were holding hands when we came to a funny looking door that looked like an elevator. He said, "just a minute," and went inside. He was gone for a long time. As I waited, the creepy people kept going by, and I was getting more worried. Finally after about 30 minutes he came tumbling out and was disheveled and bruised. I hugged him and told him how glad I was to see him. I was a little embarrassed*

that I was not sure what his name was.

The real-life circumstances are not even relevant to this dream because it could apply to any situation over which I feel persecuted or in peril. I sensed protection waking up from this dream. It seems He went into the elevator and took care of business for me. He took the beating I might have endured without him. Does this image remind you of anything? How about the Easter story?

I believe with my whole heart God sends these messages to me through the Holy Spirit when I need reassurance things will be alright. You probably have your own ups and downs (the elevator metaphor)and dream of creepy guys after you from time to time. I know you will find peace of mind by watching to see who makes an appearance in your dreams and deciphering the symbolism of how this deity acts on your behalf. Your Chief Advisor may have already shown up in your dreams without you realizing it.

Jesus also pulls me out of messes and rescues me from disaster in my sleep, just as people thousands of years ago were saved in

Biblical accounts. At a time when I had a significant personal decision to make, a nighttime vision reminded me when certain disaster seems imminent, He is there.

> My dream: *I dreamed some friends and I were going to Niagara Falls. One of them suggested we get in a car with a little old lady who appeared to know where we needed to go. We piled into the car, but soon we were all turned around trying to find our way. My friend, Cindy, grabbed the map and directed from the back seat. I looked over her shoulder, and the two of us were heavily into reading the tiny print. When I finally looked up at the driver, she was painting her nails and driving straight for the falls. Just as we teetered on the edge a "big man" threw my purse and briefcase out to me. I caught them and walked to safety.*

Sometimes the symbolism is so vivid I find myself chuckling at its obviousness. The driver, in painting her nails, represents a person leading us to the brink, focused on looking good rather than safely getting us to our destination. Immersed in detail with our noses to the map, Cindy and I missed the big picture until it was nearly too late. The dream virtually shouted at me to look at the big picture and quit being so analytical. I believe the big man—Jesus—tossed me the bag holding the answer. I just had to look to avoid falling off the edge.

I receive tips from my Chief Advisors on a regular basis, whether at home or away. Since I traveled frequently, I know nearly all hotel rooms provide a pad and pen on the nightstand so I am ready when He whispers in my ear in the middle of the night. I have hundreds of little logo pages with shorthand filling the entire notepad. As I reread all of the dreams in my journal box over the past year, I took a trip down memory lane, remembering all the places I have been.

On one particular business trip, I traveled alone to a strange city, not unusual for my work. My schedule called for me to be there for a couple nights, and the thought occurred to me that I might go out and explore the second night in town, until a dream altered my plans. I woke up night one and wrote on a hotel note pad the following:

> *I got into an SUV and drove into town. It was Kansas City in the dream, but it did not look like it. I walked through a field and a man came up and walked with me. I kept looking down, telling him I was looking for snakes. I heard they were everywhere in this town. He said it was true and told me a story about a football team that decided not to run a play because they looked at the ground and saw a huge snake on the field. I decided to go back to my vehicle. Four or five people followed me to the car. I tried to lock it when they grabbed the door. I grabbed my phone and dialed 911, and they left because they figured the police were on their way. A woman rode by on a bike and shook her finger at me, telling me this was a no-vehicle zone. I thought to myself how stupid it was to go out alone.*

Why did I not ask someone to come with me?

Kansas City is a nice city and one I traveled to frequently. What tweaked my antennae when I read the note the next morning is the city seemed like lovely Kansas City, but *it did not look like it.* The image of snakes slithering through the dream, as you know from Chapter 5, frequently signals danger or warning, especially in my personal dream imagery.

I believe the man walking with me in the field is Jesus. In the years he traveled through Galilee, he became known for telling stories, or parables, to make a point to the people of his day. In this dream he told me the story about a football team choosing a different play because of the danger on the field. I listened and took it to heart, deciding to forego my plan to venture out in the city alone. I will never know if something terrible might have happened to me, but why take the chance when not necessary?

I keep a copy of Matthew Chapter 6 at my desk. Verses 25 and 27 read, 25"Therefore I tell you, do not worry about your life, what you will eat or drink; or about your body, what you will wear. Is not life more than food and the body more than clothes? 27 "Can any one of you by worrying add a single hour to your life?"

Even though I try to faithfully live without worry, an occasional dream in which He plays a protective role is welcome comfort.

If there is ever a question of God playing a lead role in my dreams, this journal entry confirms it beyond the shadow of a doubt. I had this dream in August of 2013, in the month I started to write DreamWalker. If you miss the symbolism in this one, I refer you to the Bible, John 1:29.

> *Dreamed I was in a place where workers were lined up to go to lunch. I was learning how things work, and people were telling me where to find the break room and bathroom. I got a snack and went to a place where a guy pulled me aside and said let's go to the small room. We were hugging close to each other and he said why couldn't we have lived closer to*

each other the past few years? It was as if we had missed the opportunity to be together. I felt very comfortable with him. We had a small room—like a stable, and he was building it for somebody. A woman came in and said where are you going to get a small enough animal to put in that room? I said how about a lamb? I woke up.

John 1: ²⁹ The next day he saw Jesus coming toward him, and said, "Behold, the Lamb of God, who takes away the sin of the world!

Dreams or illusions, call them what you want.

They lift us from the commonplace of life to

better times.

~ Henry Wadsworth Longfellow

15

CONCLUSION

I cannot tell you, based on your dreams, exactly what decisions to make or how to live your life, as dream images and metaphors must be placed in context within your own circumstances. The snake in my dream may be all about an untrustworthy colleague, yet it could mean healing for you.

There are several good dream dictionaries available, and I encourage you to refer to more than one before you settle on a meaning for a specific image. Dream images have a mystical quality about them, and I suggest you not take them too literally at first. I benefited from more than thirty years' worth of dream journals, and as images repeated themselves I became certain of their meaning for me, adding them to my own dream dictionary.

I do believe that analyzing the images appearing in your dreams will boost your confidence in the decisions you make.

How many of us ever looked back years to review decisions we made and judge whether they were the right ones? We kick ourselves for the most glaring examples of regretful decisions, but how often do we critique our daily problem solving skills and tell ourselves "good job"? Memories get foggy as lives get busier with more and more stuff.

Gratefully, we tend to remember the bright spots in people and events, but it does not keep us from repeating mistakes and bad judgment calls. It is difficult to objectively analyze how we did when choosing the forks in the road—both momentous and those of less significance.

Dream journaling is a useful device for moving us along the path we call "life" without stumbling or falling too hard. It captures our deepest thoughts and messages from the Universe, turning them into practical advice usable by the attentive dreamer. I established a few practices I use to assist me in creating a journal of revelation and understanding. May I remind you of the most important:

1. Develop a habit of writing down your dreams before you get out of bed.

Equip your nightstand with everything you need to effectively journalize before your memory is interrupted. Have paper and pen handy, along with a small light, just enough to see the paper. Avoid turning on a full scale lamp, as it jars you awake and lets the thoughts escape too easily. Let your sleep partner know you will be doing this so she or he knows when to be extra quiet and let you do your thing before the dream is forgotten.

2. Practice your fast penmanship. If you are blessed with a skill like shorthand or note hand, consider using it. I only advise against it if you have a difficult time reading your own writing. Transcribing it into a typed format on a regular basis is highly recommended. Do not wait thirty years to type them out, as I did (although it is a labor of love remembering the stories behind dreams as you reread and transcribe.)

3. Capture details, details, and more details. Do not leave anything out. Include descriptions of people, places

and things with colors and names. Nothing is too small a point to include.

4. Record, along with the dream, your initial thoughts on its meaning. I write the dream down and then put *"Note:"* after it to signify the difference between the actual dream and my interpretative notes. It is also constructive to include a few words about anything going on in your life at the time. This is tremendously beneficial for me to understand the message being sent, putting it into context. Include bits and pieces from work, home and community. For example, I may write a blurb like this: *"Note: Made an important presentation today on hiring Betty Smith. Doctor's appointment to investigate recurring headaches. Met with Joey's teacher regarding his lack of interest in science."* Of course, include more detail if something significant happened. You may dream about it days or weeks later.

5. Find a trusted friend with whom you can discuss your dreams and interpret

for each other. It is not absolutely necessary to decipher the meaning, since you alone will know how to interpret it for yourself after a while. It is fun, though, to trade stories with a dream believer, and he may recognize something you missed in the imagery.

6. I recommend taking time to go back and read your journal every now and then. I observed the longer ago it happened, the richer the dream's meaning is for me. With sharp vision and perspective, it becomes clear which of my analyses missed the mark at first and which ones I "nailed." After I journaled for a few years, my interpretative accuracy improved, and it continues to get better with time. Much of my understanding is due to having finessed my dream dictionary, honing the symbolism explained in other publications to suit me. My symbols remain consistent. A snake in any of my dreams, for example, is definitely a cause for heightened awareness.

I hope you found my expedition to be encouraging. My dreams provide a way for me to handle difficult situations, solve problems, and make decisions on a little more than a gut feel. I still believe my intuition is razor sharp, but the gut-gauge feeds the little analytical voice inside me shouting, "Give me some evidence!"

My DreamWalker journey gets more intriguing as I experiment with asking more challenging questions of The Universe before I nod off to sleep. The secret is sleeping well, with the intention of spending a good deal of time in the REM stages of sleep. According to Davina MacKail, *The Dream Whisperer*, "all of our emotive, creative, solution-seeking chemicals are switched on and powered up" during the REM cycle.

Finally, I pray you will find meaningful messages in your dreams from Your Higher Power. In a world of uncertainty and shaky foundations, it is the one thing upon which you can always depend.

Blessings for a rich dream life and sleep well, my friend.

ACKNOWLEDGMENTS

Thank you, Ray Thomas, for your love and support, encouraging me to make this book happen and listening to all my crazy dreams and self analysis.

To my sister, Sandy Dunst, I send love and gratitude for always being there in life and for playing a lead role in my dreams.

To Caroline Perkins, my friend and partner in business, teaching, writing and fun, I cherish our many conversations about books and ideas. You've always been my writing role model, and I continue to learn from you.

I am grateful to the Anthem Authors of Sun City, Henderson, Nevada, for editing and mentoring, encouragement, and patience as I transformed myself from business writer to author, learning the differences along the way.

To the Critique Group, thank you for your keen eye and gentle critiques. A special thank-you to

James, Donna, MaryAnn, and Jeane for your editing skills. I've learned much from all of you.

To writing coach and mentor, Denise Michaels, thank you for getting me on the road to

publishing my work. Your insight and gentle nudging is the reason why this book became a reality. Shepherding the International Book Writing Guild networking group is your precious gift to writers all over the world.

A special thank you to Sigurd Medhus, "auditor of the auditors," for your extraordinary detail work in editing, especially at a time you were dealing with your own challenges.

I am grateful for the candid feedback and probing questions from James Logsdon early in the project to make sure my work would be understood by those who don't necessarily live in the same dream world I do.

To Nancy, Candace, Margaret, Beth, Mary Jane, Joyce, Jeane and Melody for sharing your dreams and listening to mine, I hope you find your own "aha" moments within these pages.

Thank you to Rita, who lifted me over the confidence hurdles. Your gifts are a true blessing.

For showing up as characters repeatedly in my dreams, I am grateful to Pastor Peter, Gary, John, and Pete for having an impact on me that made me understand the metaphors in my mind.

To Mom and Dad, who are reading this book from above and recognizing the times they needed to appear in my dreams, you now know the importance of your roles as my parents, and I am grateful that you still show up to look over my shoulder now and again.

To my cousin, Linda, I dedicate my dream analysis. She encouraged me as I wrote the manuscript. We enjoyed a special connection. Her open mindedness and desire to understand things beyond this world set an example for me many years ago. She would have written the Foreword, had she not passed away before I was able to publish this book.

To Dave, Juliet, Sandy, Tom, Kinsey, Max, Charlie, Michael, and Ben, I hope this book encourages you to listen to your dreams and know you will find the answers you seek.

For my Lord and Savior, Jesus Christ, who communicates with me through my dreams, I am eternally grateful for knowing you and pray that I am walking the path you intended for me.

APPENDIX

Sources

Miller, Gustavus Hindman; *10,000 Dreams Interpreted, An Illustrated Guide to Unlocking the Secrets of Your Dreamlife*, Element Books Limited 1996; text revised © Barnes & Noble, Inc. 1996.

Riggio, Ronald E. PhD, article "Women's Intuition: Myth or Reality," Cutting Edge Leadership, *Psychology Today,* July 14, 2011.

Crisp, Tony; *Dream Dictionary, An A to Z Guide To Understanding Your Unconscious Mind;* Dell Publishing, division of Bantam Doubleday Dell Publishing Group, Inc.

Web site, www.achievement.org, Academy of Achievement, interview, Salk, Jonas; accessed August, 2013.

Web site, *www.dreammoods*.com, Dream Moods, Inc. Dream Dictionary; accessed April, 2013.

Lauri Quinn Loewenberg, *Dream On It, Unlock Your Dreams, Change Your Life,* copyright 2011 by Loewenberg, Inc. d/b/a The Dream Zone, St. Martin's Press.

Web site, *www.Dreamforth.com*, accessed May, 2013.

Crisp, Tony; web site *www.Dreamhawk.com*, Discussion Forum, accessed April-May, 2013.

Glanville, John G; web site *www.Dreaminterpretation-dictionary.com*, accessed April-June, 2013.

Flora, Carlin; article "Gut Almighty," *Psychology Today*, published May 1, 2007; last reviewed May 11, 2012.

Web site *www.MyTherapyJournal.com*, accessed August, 2013.

Dale, Cyndi, *The Subtle Body: An Encyclopedia of Your Energetic Anatomy,* www.cyndidale.com, copyright 2009 Cyndi Dale.

Huntsman, Joy; web site www.MyTherapyJournal.com, accessed August, 2013.*www.joyandassociates.com*, accessed August, 2013.

Web site *www.Sleepculture.com*, accessed June, 2013.

The Holy Bible, King James Version, A Regency Bible from Thomas Nelson Publishers, 1990.

Turner, Rebecca, interview with Dr. Keith Hearne, Ph.D., www.world-of-lucid-dreaming.com, accessed June, 2014.

WebMD News Archive, *Creative People Remember More Dreams,* June 27, 2003; sources: *Personality and Individual Differences,* May 2003. News release, University of Iowa.

Women's Devotional Bible, New International Version, copyright 1990, 1994 The Zondervan Corporation.

MacKail, Davina; *The Dream Whisperer, Unlock the Power of Your Dreams*, Hay House, Inc., copyright Davina MacKail, 2010.

Garfield, Patricia, Ph.D., *The Universal Dream Key, The 12 Most Common Dream Themes Around the World*; HarperCollins Publishers, Inc., 2001.

MY CUSTOM DREAM DICTIONARY

Calling a dream dictionary "custom" is a bit of an oxymoron, since everyone's dictionary is customized. A certain image in your dream may mean something completely different from that same person, place or thing that appears in my dreams. To provide context for the examples I included in *DreamWalker: Use Your Dreams to Make Confident Life Decisions*, I share my personal dream dictionary, crafted over decades of analyzing and learning to recognize images' meanings to me.

Airplane, flights	General venue for many activities; airplane crashing or diving represents danger or problems
Beach	A desirable place to be
Boat	Opportunity or the point of the matter; "missed the boat" meaning a lost opportunity; someone did not understand the primary point

Bridge	Making a transition from one place to another or a life change such as a job
Church	A group of believers in a strategy, a thought or a person
Congress, senator, Washington, DC	Politics coming into play
Elevator	Path to a higher level of achievement or success; could also represents ups and downs in life
Feet sticking up on the beach	People who have "their heads in the sand;" missing an important point, not seeing things clearly, naive
Fire	Transformation; letting go of the old, making room for new growth
Flying without a plane	Success, achievement

Flying with feet hitting buildings	Obstacles preventing success
Going to the bathroom	Relieving myself of a burden or problem resolution
Golf course setting; tee it up; hazards	Playing or working in a man's world
Hugging	The person hugging me is on my side, a sign of trust, empathy
Jewelry	Something treasured, rewards for success, achievement; trying to look good; spiritual goodness; wisdom and riches
Lamb	Jesus
Luggage, baggage	Impediment to progress; a figurative weight carried on my shoulders
Moving in and out of offices	Transition in life or work

Naked	Exposure to risk or embarrassment
Orchestra or band setting; missing instrument or music	A performance taking place such as a presentation at work; missing instrument signifies a tool or resource not in place or something I forgot; missing music represents a lack of guidance or instructions
Parents	Good conscience, judgment
Pastor	Protective, comforting, generally a reference to God/Jesus, a higher power
Pink	Immaturity, weakness, not a favorable color
Purse	Something of value, whether tangible or intangible
Roller coaster	Instability
Smoking, smoker	Need to stay away from

Snake	Snake in the grass, person who presents himself to be a good person, but secretly is out to get me
Making a presentation and unprepared	Not prepared for something important, a call to pay attention;
Teal	Loyal, trustworthy, favorable color
Vomiting	Do not "have the stomach" for whatever is going on
Water	Deep or coming over a bridge means "up to my neck" in an issue
Wheels coming off, out of shape on car or bike	Warning
Windy	Change taking place
Yellow	Caution, risk; illness

Made in the USA
Middletown, DE
29 August 2015